Making Writing Work for You

HAROLD L. TAYLOR

MAKING WRITING WORK *for* YOU

Copyright ©2024 Harold L. Taylor

First Edition

Print ISBN: 978-1-7382942-5-1

eBook ISBN: 978-1-7382942-6-8

10 9 8 7 6 5 4 3

Editor: Don Loney
Proofreader: Jill Attack
Interior Design: Kevin Coleman
Cover art: Biserka Design

Contents

Introduction

By way of introduction, here is my writing career in a nutshell. I have loved writing since I was a kid. By the time I reached high school, I was selling the odd filler. Much later I discovered the greeting card market and started writing greeting card ideas. The greeting card companies paid more and were fun to do. After I finished high school I signed up for a *Writer's Digest* correspondence course to see if I could write short stories, but I never finished the course. I still wonder if not completing the course had any bearing on never having my short stories accepted for publication. But a few editors were kind enough to send me rejection letters accompanied by suggestions for improving my writing, which I never heeded—one of my many mistakes on my journey as a writer.

By the time I graduated college and had worked for a few years, I had a few hundred greeting card ideas and other fillers such as short verse, epigrams, and anecdotes to my credit. I eventually switched to nonfiction and started writing articles, leaving the filler market behind. I sold some, but most of the articles were accepted by non-paying newspapers and magazines. During my twelve years in industry and eight years teaching management courses at a community college, I continued writing articles and started my own association management business.

Part of my business involved writing newsletters and publishing a magazine for a client. After some reflection, I decided to purchase two trade magazines, *Canadian Clay & Ceramics* and *Sales & Marketing Management in Canada*. Then I started a fourth magazine from scratch. I called it *The Ceramic Hobbyist*. Of course, as editor/publisher, I must admit (unsurprisingly) I accepted everything I wrote. But my "Keys to Effective Management" column won an award from the Business Press Editor's Association for outstanding editorial achievement in the Professional Development Series category—proof evidently that my work had some quality, which I took as a sign to keep writing.

I eventually wrote my first book, which was on time management. (I had started speaking and presenting seminars on the topic of time management and needed a book to build my credibility.) The book, *Making Time Work for You*, became a Canadian bestseller. That's when my part-time writing started paying off, both financially and career-wise. My business website, blog articles, time management newsletter, social media presence, back of the room sales at my workshops and speeches, all helped sales of anything I wrote. My writing was then working for me. Ten years later I had seven books published through traditional publishing houses and around the same number of self-published titles.

My seminars on time management prompted me to incorporate a second business, Harold Taylor Time Consultants Ltd. I sold the original company, Harold L Taylor Enterprises Ltd., to my staff so I could focus on my training and speaking. While writing had been a part-time activity and could never support me, let alone a family, it did launch my reputation as a professional speaker and time management trainer, and I did exceptionally well in that field.

A.J. Harper, in her book *Write a Must-Read*, admits that publishing a book will help grow your business, but advises against using it as a business card. To quote her, "Your book is not a better business card. Why would you want that? People throw business cards away."

I wrote the book precisely because people don't throw books away, as they do with business cards. If companies enquired about my workshops and keynotes, I included the book with the promotional package consisting of a bio, rates, client list, referrals, clips from newspaper coverage of my events, testimonials, and information on my programs. If a prospective client even glanced through the book, they would see suggestion after suggestion on how to manage their time more effectively (the same suggestions that they would get in my presentations). My speaking engagements doubled within the year and in the name of time management I had to increase my fees.

The big mistake that I see being made by speakers and trainers is being afraid of giving away all their "good stuff" in a book. That is what prevents authors from writing the "great book" that Harper refers to. There's nothing wrong with using a book to promote your business or career. It's no different than writing a book to make money from the book. If it's not a good book, you won't make a significant amount of money from it either way.

My "business card" book, *Making Time Work for You*, created from articles and initially used to promote my speaking career, became a Canadian bestseller quickly because of the promotion efforts of the publisher. It was released in hardcover simultaneously in Toronto by General Publishing and New York by Beaufort. It was translated into five languages and published in fourteen countries. Dell published it as a mass-market pocketbook, and SMI in Waco, Texas released it as an audiobook. It was later released in different softcover formats and as part of a business book series. The fact that I traveled and spoke frequently, and the publisher lined up interviews with radio, TV stations and newspapers everywhere I went, made a huge difference. When the book became outdated and was declared out-of-print, I took back the rights, updated it, added new material and sold it from my website and at conferences, and decades later I included the book in many of my workshops. May it now rest in peace.

I do recommend A.J. Harper's book, because it's a much better book than I could write, but I want to clarify that point about business cards. It's likely the case that many readers of this book will be speakers, trainers, organizers, and others whose prime business is not writing, but who would like to use writing to promote their business. If so, you don't have to be a book-length work. You can promote your business by writing articles and blog posts. You might refer to my eBook *How to Write Articles for Self-Promotion* published by Bookboon, a Denmark-based publisher, which has published forty-four of my books in eBook formats. (I discuss articles in a later chapter.)

After several years of writing fillers for various magazines and greeting cards, I have focused on writing for business audiences primarily on time management and leadership, self-development, and soft skills. I continue to write short treatments of topics related to time management, which include a publication for the Christian market titled *God-Centered Time Management*, which won a 2022 Word Guild award for best book in the "instructional" category.

I also write weekly devotionals for the church I attend, a biweekly blog article for my website (although I regularly fail to be regular), a quarterly newsletter, and until recently, a biweekly column for our local *Kings County Record* newspaper.

I still love writing, and yes, sometimes I regret not having followed my original plan to take journalism in college instead of Research Technology and to have experienced the life of a struggling full-time writer. But then I wouldn't have learned all that I have learned over the years, or had a successful speaking business, or been able to share the information with you in this book.

I recall as a youngster I was asked this question by an editor who returned one of my short stories: "Why don't you experience life before you start writing about it?" I was upset when I received that comment over sixty years ago, but I now realize it was good advice. You can't draw water from an empty well.

Most of what I know now I learned through trial and error, which included plenty of errors and rejections. And frankly, I have enjoyed the comfortable life of a part-time writer. It now leaves me with a part-time writing job during my retirement years—one that is enjoyable, rewarding, and allows me plenty of time for volunteering. As I write this introduction, I am about to turn ninety, and still mobile, healthy, and enjoying life. And I attribute much of that to writing, which not only stimulates the brain, but also provides the income needed to travel and to continue the lifestyle that I have been blessed to enjoy throughout my working life.

I urge you to be on the lookout for the hint of a "gift of writing" that is evident in the lives of so many successful full-time writers. This allows you to change your career at any point in your life. It's nice to have that option.

I have enjoyed being a part-time writer, without fame or fortune, or invasion of privacy, or the expectations of others that usually come with being a celebrity author. Let me share with you some of my experiences and what I have learned over the years as a part-time writer. It is even possible for those who have no evidence of a "gift of writing." Writing is a skill that almost anyone can develop. You can become a successful writer if you have a gift, a talent, or a skill for writing. The gift is given, the talent can be nurtured, and the skill can be developed. You don't need all three.

Almost anyone can be a writer, regardless of background, training, or career. The knowledge you acquire in formal education is useless if you don't use it. The value of knowledge is in the implementation. Grades are great in the short term to get you through school or into a job, but they don't help in the long term to keep the job or be successful at whatever you do. What you don't use, you lose.

I have a certificate on my closet wall that says I have a good grade in a three-year evening course in ceramic technology from McMaster University. But I now know very little, if anything, about ceramics, and I would certainly not qualify for a job in the glass or ceramics business. I also have a three-year diploma, complete with each year's grade in research technology from Ryerson Institute of Technology, but I wouldn't know where to start if I were to work in a research lab. I have nothing on that wall that qualifies me to teach, yet I spent eight years as a teaching master at Humber College in Toronto with fair success. It's not the grade—it's using and practicing what you study that is of value. The same goes for writing. A writer must write, and again and again.

The good news is that most of us, regardless of our background or studies or careers, have been writing in one form or another, whether that was in our jobs, diaries, journals, or personal correspondence. And writers mentioned in this book came from various backgrounds and careers that had little to do with writing. But they had a story to tell or information to pass on to others, and they put it in writing. Eventually, through practice and persistence, they were published—again and again.

So, why not you?

Chapter 1

Are You Meant to Be a Writer?

Were you born to write? I ask this question because so many people catch the writing bug as kids and then are diverted away from writing into other careers by the well-meaning advice of others or by circumstance. I was advised to pursue an education in research technology, not journalism. "Journalism doesn't pay," I was informed. "The future is in plastics. Get a job with DuPont or CIL or one of those companies."

The advice made sense at the time, I thought, and I only had to work one year after high school to get enough money for the tuition at Ryerson Institute of Technology in Toronto and take the three-year course in research technology at its School of Chemistry.

Thus the desire to write became dimmer the busier I became at my part-time jobs in Toronto at Griffiths Laboratories and Loblaws while going through school. But periodically I would still write and managed to get a few items published. My little time devoted to writing was devoured by my career path at Canadian Johns-Manville, then American-Standard, and Humber College, and eventually by my own businesses.

It was not until I practiced what I preached in my talks and seminars on time management that I had the time to write part-time on a regular basis. But in my senior years, after I downsized my business and stopped flying around North America speaking and presenting workshops on time management, my writing, in one form or another, finally consumed most of my time. Semi-retirement has been the most enjoyable and productive time of my life. I try not to think about my life if I had followed my initial innate passion to write. But I'm not the only one to be called a late bloomer. I am one of many who have ignored their calling—if indeed I had been "called" at all.

Is It Ever Too Late to Begin Writing?

One example of a late bloomer came to my notice recently when I saw a headline in the April 2024 issue of *The Epoch Times*, in El Monte, California: "Columnist, 101, delights readers with hometown stories." It was written by Randy Tatano, and it concerned a 101-year-old man in an assisted-living facility in Monroeville, Alabama who didn't start writing until he was in his seventies. He was distracted from his calling until he sold his business and began looking for something to do in retirement.

I'm assuming he had that same spark for writing that I experienced at the age of twelve. The thing is, at that age his teacher accused him of having his mother write an essay for him because he was not smart enough to have written it himself. And as the writer of the article said, his creative talent lay dormant for more than sixty years. The gentleman's name is George Jones, and he shows no sign of slowing down in his writing, although he has been slowed down by his walker.

I'm still mobile at ninety and am inspired by this man of 101 who finally wrote an unpublished novel at age ninety-four. And I'm also grateful I had time during my busiest years to have had many short verses, anecdotes, and greeting card ideas published, as well as several books and hundreds of articles. And my most productive years as a part-time writer have been in the past decade.

As individuals, we don't develop a mission; we discover it, according to the late Richard Bolles, author of *What Color Is Your Parachute?*. He claimed that "When we search for a sense of mission, we are searching for reassurance that the world is a little bit richer for our being here, and a little poorer after our going." He believed that we are put on this earth for a purpose, and it is up to us to discover what that purpose is. If we are born with a purpose, we should have some indication of that purpose in our earlier years, even though we may not be fully aware of it at the time.

And this tends to be the case. Denis Waitley, in his book, *The New Dynamics of Goal Setting*, talks about a series of British films that followed the lives of fifty people from the age of seven to the age of thirty-five. Most of the individuals eventually found work that was related to their childhood interests, even after straying from those interests as young adults.

You may have noticed that many people who retire make a full-time job out of what used to be a hobby or interest—one that they didn't have the time to pursue, or what a well-meaning counselor or parent had diverted them from because it didn't seem like a viable option as a well-paying career. But I wonder—a lot—about how many gifted writers have failed to latch onto this gift that has been given to them—the facility to write. So if you are reading

4

this book and don't know if you have a natural talent to write, think back to your childhood. Did you enjoy your English class more when you were asked to write stories or essays, or describe a nature scene or whatever? Perhaps you had a natural way with words and were able to find rhymes easily or to imagine a storyline, or had an ability to pronounce words phonetically? Did you like to read or listen to stories, or tell "make believe" stories to other kids or keep a diary? Any of these could be a clue that you are destined to write.

If so, bring this innate talent to the surface by intentionally reading and writing every chance you get. Register for a writing course of some kind. Hang out with others who have the same interests. Continue to take self-development courses as you grow older. You have a lifetime (or what's left of it) ahead of you, so make use of it. If you should decide to do something else, the skills of writing and communication will assist you in whatever field you choose. It will not be time wasted.

Consider Starting as a Part-Time Writer

Even successful full-time writers like John Grisham and Stephen King started out as part-time writers. Grisham wrote between meetings and court appearances, and King at one time took a job in an industrial laundry and continued to write stories in his spare time. If you want to be a writer badly enough, you will find the time to write.

I believe John Grisham has the gift, but it didn't break free until he was a lawyer and he felt the need to write a book inspired by a court case he was watching. This doesn't mean it suddenly became easy to make a living by writing. His first book, *A Time to Kill*—and one that was rejected by many publishers—was not suddenly transformed into a much better book. It was the same book that later became a bestseller, a movie, and a top money-maker when his second book, *The Firm*, suddenly took off. Persistence is one of the secrets of success for most writers, as we will see as we go along.

If you don't have the innate gift of writing, you don't have to become another John Grisham, Stephen King, or J.K. Rowling. You can still become a successful full-time writer. Or you can settle for being a part-time writer like I have been for most of my life, and easily earn thousands of dollars annually or monthly to supplement your present income, whether you are employed or retired. Your earnings depend on how much time you want to invest in writing. With a little luck on your side, you may earn more than a million dollars writing part-time during your lifetime without giving up your full-time job.

But don't give up your day job right away, even if you discover that your gift is writing. If you're already retired, of course, you can't lose. I love to write and I will continue to write whether I get paid or not.

If you do decide to be a writer, don't put it off. Make it a priority, even if that means writing as soon as you wake up in the morning. Many writers do other tasks first, and delay writing until the very last minute, according to Frank Partnoy, in his book *Wait: The Useful Art of Procrastination*. He says that George Ainsley, the impatient scholar, said that procrastination is harder to quit than alcohol or drug addiction.

But let me tell you some of the things I have learned as a part-time writer. It will include a way of solving the procrastination dilemma—at least when it comes to writing.

Chapter 2

Make Writing a Habit

Build a habit of writing every day, whether it's a goal of one hundred words a day as recommended by David Kadavy in his book *100-Word Writing Habit: A Small Action with Big Results*, or one thousand words a day as suggested by Jami Attenberg in her book *1000 Words: A Writer's Guide to Staying Creative, Focused, and Productive All Year Round.* The number of words is not as important as the regularity of time devoted to writing. Habits are formed by repetition, not quantity. The more times you write, the faster the habit is formed.

You might have a target of one thousand words a day as John Grisham does, for instance, or be happy with an output of one hundred words every single day. You will not only develop a habit but will produce a lot of words, which are the building blocks of books, articles, newsletters, social media posts, short stories, eBooks, scripts, essays, and so on.

Octavia Butler, author of *Bloodchild and Other Stories,*

gives some good advice in Virginia Ann Byrd's book *I'm Still Writing*: "Don't rely on inspiration. Habit is dependable," she claims. She goes on to say, "Habit will help you finish your stories, but inspiration won't."

The important thing is to write every day, and if possible, to do so at the same time and place. Writing during idle moments in waiting rooms, airports, commuting, or when meetings are canceled, are bonus times, but they are not the most productive times. This advice assumes you are only a part-time writer. If you decide to write full time, your schedule may indeed change. You might write for two or even three ninety-minute blocks of time a day with breaks in between, but don't overdo it. Full-time writing does not need to exclude time spent with family, friends, travel, and recreation, and on other commitments.

Kadavy says that despite most people thinking a few thousand words is a good daily goal, he doesn't agree. He claims that you might hit the one-thousand-word mark the first day or so you put pen to paper (or fingers to keyboard) for a couple of weeks if you're self-disciplined. But when you miss a day or two it becomes even harder to continue with such an optimistic goal.

He has a point. But based on my time management background and experience, if you schedule time instead of words, and make it a habit to spend ninety minutes per day writing, it doesn't matter how many words you write. You will always reach your goal. Why? Because the goal is ninety minutes, and most people can focus on a task for ninety minutes. It frees you from the stress of having to produce a specific word count. If you write one hundred words, and they're really good, then the ninety minutes has been very well spent. I can usually write more than a thousand words in an hour-and-a-half, especially since I write in the early morning, free from interruptions or distractions. Do what works for you; the important thing is to make it a habit.

How to Become a Top-Performing Writer

You have probably heard of the 10,000-hour rule popularized by Malcolm Gladwell in his book *Outliers: The Story of Success*, and the concept of "deliberate practice" necessary to become an elite performer in your chosen field of expertise. If not, the bibliography at the end of this book will bring you up to date. (Or read my eBook, *How to Be a Top Performer*, published by Bookboon.)

"Deliberate practice" refers to doing something with energy, commitment, and focus. It's not simply a matter of reading, hearing, viewing, and repeating information mindlessly or automatically. Regardless of how many times you do something, you will only succeed in being able to do it habitually at a less-than-great level. With rote practice you can become a decent writer, golfer, carpenter, violinist, manager, or whatever, but you will never achieve a level of greatness in a field. However if you are willing to put in the hours (at least 10,000 over a period of ten years or more according to research, most of which is based on the findings of researcher Anders Ericsson) and apply the suggestions of others mentioned, you will succeed.

You don't have to put your life on hold while you do this. Life goes on regardless, and if you desire to excel in any job, skill, or profession, and love doing it, you have nothing to lose even if it takes a lifetime to achieve your goal. You may balk when the figure "ten years" is mentioned, but would you rather be a mediocre writer or author with an income and reputation to match in ten years, or an elite author earning millions? Time passes at the same pace either way.

With deliberate or purposeful practice, you must never rush, but instead calmly and mindfully review instructional materials and practice repeatedly, adjusting each time you receive feedback so you can continually improve. It is best to enlist the help of an instructor or at least an outside observer who can identify areas or elements that can be improved. You need a goal to work towards.

Christine Carter, in her book *The Sweet Spot: How to Find Your Groove at Home and Work*, writes that mastery of any task or activity requires three things: (1) grit (or passion, persistence); (2) rest; and (3) good coaching and great teachers. Most would agree that it is difficult to master anything without the assistance of a teacher, trainer, mentor, or coach, who can observe, offer feedback, and guide you.

Mastering a task or skill is not synonymous with top performance. To achieve top performance, you must never stop trying to improve. Be creative and have no fear of taking risks. When people get really good at something, they are in their comfort zone and so they lose the drive to improve. As Ericsson says, getting out of your comfort zone means trying to do something that you couldn't do before. When you succeed at this new task you have the confidence to tackle another. Your skills and talents begin to measure up to top performance.

You might be a hockey fan, or not, but I have watched the game since I was a toddler (and even played a little). But the things players do on the ice now seem supernatural. In particular I watch Mitch Marner, who plays for the Toronto Maple Leafs. He, as well as other top players, such as his teammate William Nylander, score goals in ways rarely attempted by players in recent memory. As Marner skates in on a goalie, I've seen him pass the puck between his legs from back to front and retrieve it, approach the goal from the left side and do a complete 360-degree spin, and while the baffled goalie is wondering what's going on, finish the turn by slipping the puck into the opposite corner of the net. He will pass the puck to an empty space on the ice—sometimes without looking—where a teammate steams into view and captures the puck. Today players bat the puck into the net as though their hockey stick is a baseball bat, and others literally pick up the puck with the blade of their stick and tuck it into the top corner of the net.

But occasionally they have looked like idiots by losing the puck or having the pass intercepted by the other team. That's the danger of taking risks and trying new things, but that's also what makes for growth and greatness. Top performers are not just trying harder, they are also trying things differently. They do things that have never been done before. I think that's what Ericsson meant by purposeful practice. I would wager that Marner and other elite players spend many hours privately practicing these new maneuvers. I'm not sure whether it adds up to the thousand hours or not, but it gets results.

After including the above information on Marner in my book *How to Be a Top Performer*, I read an article by Mike Zeisberger that confirms the effort that Marner puts into his practice. He has had a coach since he was four years old. Robert Desveaux, who runs 3 Zones Hockey School in Durham, Ontario, has worked with Marner for the past two decades. He was quoted as saying, "Marner's drive for improvement never stops." As a smaller player as a child, Marner built resilience by having a coach use pads to knock him down in a corner of the rink. He would bounce back up again and always with a smile on his face.

William Nylander was also coached at a young age. His father was an NHL player, and Nylander probably logged more than ten thousand hours of focused training in order to become great. Innate talent is not enough. If you want to go from good to great it takes practice, commitment, and training.

Although most performance coaching books focus on athletes, the principles apply to writers as well. Writing every day, whether it is one hundred or two thousand words, will eventually make you a top writer or author. But you must be a student as well, always learning, always submitting your work to whoever will accept it whether there is payment involved or not, and always accepting advice and criticism graciously, and continuing to read more than you write.

It's up to you. The best time for you to start if you haven't already started is now. Being able to take rejections in stride is part of the training. Athletes don't escape bumps and injuries on the way to success. And writers normally experience bumps and injuries to their pride and motivation along the way to becoming a successful writer.

Consider Joining a Writers' Group

There are probably varying opinions on this, but I suggest joining a writers' group or two. It may help you become a top performer. Most groups provide feedback on your writing and provide an opportunity for you to read your material out loud. (If you stumble over your own words, perhaps it's because of your injudicious choice of words or the incorrect way they are used.) It might also be a great environment for testing something new and creative. You need feedback as well as coaching to become a top writer. I've heard complaints that some groups never tell the truth and are simply mutual admiration societies. But if you are not happy, you can always move to another group, or start one of your own. There's nothing wrong with sharing your goals and getting a little encouragement. And some groups have knowledgeable guest speakers, workshops, a lending library of books on writing, and so on.

The most important benefit of joining a writers' group is the feedback, but only if it is given properly. I'm a subscriber to the rule that we need four positive comments on our work to each critical one. Many writers tend to interpret advice as criticism, but it has been shown that even giving only positive feedback can improve an individual's writing. One example of this appeared in a book by Joyce Cooper-Kahn and Margaret Foster, *Boosting Executive Skills in the Classroom*. Margaret attended a writers' workshop that included an assignment to write a rough draft of a story for fifteen minutes and then exchange their stories with others in the group. Then the participants provided feedback on the story given to them. There was a special requirement. All of the feedback had to be positive. Margaret thought that providing only positive feedback would result in superficially making the participants feel better, but by the end of the four days together, each of the participants' writing had improved substantially. The explanation, confirmed by the writers, was that when receiving feedback on things that people liked best about their writing, each day they would work harder on whatever readers seemed to like. Evidently, doing more of what they already did well improved their writing. Positive feedback is not lightweight.

Yet another benefit of joining a writers' group is the accountability to others to attend meetings and have additional work to share, not to mention the time spent with other aspiring writers. When you work and write alone in an apartment every day like I do, getting together with colleagues once or twice a month is a big plus.

Chapter 3

The 90-Minute Rule

When I write, I follow the procedure that I recommend in my time management books and articles. I work in ninety-minute segments of time, followed by a half-hour "break." The break is necessary to dispense with email, listen to voicemail messages, etc., and to stretch or go for a brief walk. Working longer than ninety minutes without a break makes it more difficult to maintain focus, depletes your energy faster, and makes you more susceptible to both external and self-interruptions.

I'm a lark or early bird. I get in my first ninety-minute session before breakfast, which means a six-thirty start. That might be the only time I work on a writing project that day. And ninety minutes might be all the time you are able to salvage if you're only a part-time writer. I have a target of publishing four titles a year with Bookboon, and four turns out to be the average number of books I have published with that company over the last ten years.

Since the early 1980s I have always scheduled projects

and tasks in about ninety-minute segments. In my first book, *Making Time Work for You*, first published in 1981, I referred to it as my time policy. Originally, it was simply because I found I was less productive if I worked beyond ninety minutes. Since then, I have accumulated a long list of reasons why working in ninety-minute chunks is more effective. And it fits well in this digital age of speed. Today's environment is riddled with external interruptions that would decimate your personal productivity if you allow them to be an immediate priority.

Also, concentration rises and falls in ninety-minute cycles, and I find that ninety minutes is about the maximum time that I can fully concentrate on the task at hand. Taking a break after ninety minutes means you can deal with those pesky emails and text messages. Ninety minutes is not an unrealistic amount of time to be unavailable to others, so you can safely avoid most interruptions for a full ninety minutes at any time of the day. And at six-thirty in the morning, I doubt that anyone will interrupt you unless it's the kids or the family pet.

Ninety-minute segments allow two or more major writing sessions or other projects to be scheduled each day, with enough "break time" time between working sessions to handle those "urgent" emails, text messages, and other potential interruptions. How many sessions you write in a day is up to you and of course must take into account other demands on your time.

Ninety minutes allows "prime time" for at least two focused working sessions a day. This is usually in the morning, when most people that I have talked to experience their peak energy level and are more mentally alert. (They also fit the typical day's schedule for any full-time worker, consisting of two sessions of "deep work" in the morning and one in the afternoon.) The expression "deep work" was first used by Cal Newport in his book by the same title, *Deep Work: Rules for Focused Success in a Distracted World*. It refers to highly-focused work when you give your undivided attention to the task at hand. As I mentioned, my ninety minutes of focused writing before breakfast is sometimes all the writing for publication that I do that day.

> ### *Dealing with Email*
>
> *I always check my email before I start to write in the morning, so I'm free to focus on what I am doing rather than what I might be missing. This avoids the Zeigarnik Effect, Fear of Missing Out (FOMO), my natural curiosity, and lessens other brain-based time wasters. For a full explanation of why this is true, you could refer to my eBook* Always Check Email in the Morning and Other Brain-Based Strategies. *But I will mention all of them briefly in a later chapter. FOMO is also covered in more detail in chapter 15.*

I recommend you choose your writing time based on your chronotype, meaning whether you are a lark, night owl, or somewhere in between. You can determine this by trial and error.

I'm obviously an early bird or lark. I get up at five-thirty, dispense with email between six and six-thirty, and then write for ninety minutes until eight. Then I have breakfast, followed of course by another half-hour break before starting my regular job, which at this stage in my life is mostly volunteer work. This schedule has become a routine. Routines are great because they consume less energy and require less self-discipline once they are firmly entrenched.

Most successful writers seem to do something similar. They work at the same place at the same time every day and most seem to start early. Maeve Binchy, in her book *The Maeve Binchy Writers' Club* suggests, "Try to write at the same time every day; this seems to trigger the subconscious into readiness." Stephen King writes at the same time in the same place every day. In his book, *On Writing Well*, he says that mornings are his prime writing time. He claims, "If I don't write every day, the characters begin to stale off in my mind—they begin to seem like characters instead of real people." He blocks out interruptions and distractions, closes the window blinds and silences the telephone. He uses music to create his own writing world.

John Grisham only works five mornings a week. He usually starts at seven-thirty or a little later. John Updike wrote for three hours each morning, and Philip Roth started writing at ten in the morning, according to Mason Currey in his book *Daily Rituals: How Artists Work*. Laura Leist, author of *Eliminating the Chaos at Work: 25 Techniques to Increase Productivity,* told me that her favorite time to write is early in the morning when there are no distractions.

Tony Schwartz, in his book *The Way We Are Working Isn't Working*, agrees that writing in ninety-minute segments, each followed by purposeful rest, increased his productivity. A human's energy rises and falls in ninety-minute cycles called ultradian rhythms, which are an extension of the ninety-minute sleep cycles.

I don't recommend using the Pomodoro technique, which suggests working on projects for twenty-five minutes at a time with five minutes between sessions. The Pomodoro technique is not a good idea for writers, authors, or office workers. Working for only twenty-five minutes at a time leaves too many beginnings poorly started and endings unfinished. That may be good for memorizing information, but not for getting a lot done in a working environment.

Francesco Cirillo developed the Pomodoro technique as a university student. That's how it got its name. Pomodoro is a sauce made from tomatoes and he called his study "technique" after the tomato-shaped kitchen timer he used. It spawned a variety of timers. (Now you need only use your smartphone if you want to know when five minutes, twenty-five, or ninety minutes have passed.)

Admittedly, the best way for students to retain information is to space out the learning over shorter periods of time. It's called the "spacing effect" and beats long, drawn-out study sessions hands down. It also helps to memorize information in smaller chunks. When memorizing a list of facts or figures, we can recall the first and last ones better than the ones in the middle. Having more beginnings and endings helps improve memory, but this advantage disappears when you are writing or working on other tasks.

And twenty-five minutes is usually not enough time to develop "deep work" and certainly not enough time to achieve Mihaly Csikszentmihalyi's state of "flow," which some writers say they obtain when writing for longer periods of time. Flow is a state of focus so intense that you are immune to distractions.

Alan Lakein's "Swiss cheese" method for getting things done, as described in his book *How to Get Control of Your Time and Your Life*, involves working on major tasks five minutes at a time. Chipping away at a project or task until it looks like a Swiss cheese is fine when taking advantage of idle time in waiting rooms, airports, or commuting by subway or taxis, but not during office hours. They may have worked well when they were first suggested, but in Alan Lakein's time (1970s) there were no internet, smartphones, or other digital devices in use and the research of today was not available to him. And Cirillo (1980s) and his twenty-five-minute chunks of time also didn't have to contend with information doubling almost every day as we now experience.

The Coffee Shop: A Writer's Haven

There are advantages to working in coffee shops. Coffee shops are open early and most are equipped with Wi-Fi. There are no trophies or family photographs to distract you. There are few interruptions and no office gossip or morning sports updates being poured into your ear. And with a little self-discipline you can ignore email and silence your smartphone.

Some coffee shops even have better lighting than offices. And a University of Michigan study showed that people with windows facing the outside world are more productive, healthier, and maintain higher levels of concentration. People in windowless offices such as the common cubicle layout, daydream more.

According to the February 2010 issue of *Scientific American Mind*, background noise at home, work, or school not only disrupts a person's concentration, but it also increases stress levels and conditions such as high blood pressure, coronary disease, peptic ulcers, and migraine headaches.

Researchers have found that adding white noise to a classroom can be just as effective as drugs at aiding learning among ADHD pupils, so all background noise is not bad. Research carried out at the University of Illinois on the effects of background noise on creativity found that the level of noise experienced in a bustling coffee shop enhanced performance and even helped people concentrate. And according to a peer-reviewed study out of the University of Chicago, "A moderate level of ambient noise is conducive to creative cognition." A little distraction helps you to be more creative.

I find that other people surrounding me give me more energy, and yet they do not interrupt me. Sometimes I am working in what Csikszentmihalyi calls flow and I lose track of time and place. It has sometimes caused me to miss lunch.

You can visit **Coffitivity.com** and download the sounds of a coffee shop or other busy place to complement your working environment. Coffitivity recreates the ambient sounds of a cafe to boost your creativity and help you work better. But I prefer the real thing—and real coffee (as in not the virtual kind) tastes better as well!

When I had a full-time job, large portions of my books and dozens of articles were written in coffee shops during the morning rush hour. I'm not sure if I was any more creative, but I found I could get more done in a coffee shop than in a bustling office, and the walk to and from my office provided me with a much-needed dose of exercise and a creative break.

And not to forget a final important point—coffee is thought to improve your memory and energy level as well.

Chapter 4

A Writer's Library—More than the Sum of Its Parts

Prolific writers are usually avid readers and build a library of their own over the years. I prepare to write a book by buying every book on my current topic that I can get my hands on. I need to know which books and authors my new book is going to compete against. Some published ideas may be worth revisiting (with appropriate credit given) and some may not. I always check the sources of citations, the bibliography, and "For Further Reading," because some of these titles may be worthy of study.

I spent over forty years as a speaker and trainer in time management. Before I specialized in time management, I had a larger toolbox as I was providing training in about a dozen business topics. What I learned was that you cannot become a top performer in everything. You need to keep up to date with the changing environment and latest research in your area of expertise. As a result, I have accumulated many books on time management over the years. At the peak of my speaking career I had over one thousand books that had time management as the main theme, and one book was dated back to 1910. It was *How to Live on 24 Hours a Day* by Arnold Bennett. I kept my library current and that adds up to a lot of books. But I was hoping to have a long career in time management as well—and I did.

Now, ask yourself from a reader's standpoint, "Does anybody really need another book on time management telling us about the same stuff in a different way?" The answer might be, "Not unless it also contains something new that I don't know about which might be helpful to me." But speakers and trainers, including me, always feel compelled to write books and training materials. Part of that compulsion has a sound business rationale—warm leads would be led to think we know what we're talking about. Those resources lent credibility to what we had to offer. They make for an impressive business card, and they do drive new business. (Royalties are just icing on the cake.) If a publisher for some reason wasn't receptive to publishing our thought-leadership, we would simply self-publish. And the cost of the book is a legitimate expense when it is tax time.

Most top authors have writing in their blood. The gifted ones, and many of those who have successfully developed the skill, would write even if they weren't paid to do so.

Books Are My Writing Partners

Good writers are always learning so I surround myself with books. They are my inspiration, references, and friends. The topics are identified by placing different colored stickers on the spines. I try to keep similar topics together, but if one strays to another shelf, it is easily identified by the color of the dot and returned to its home base.

Scanning my bookcases will spot the ones I need for a writing project, and I move those to my desk temporarily for convenience until the project is complete. Then they are switched with others relating to my next project, and so on. It currently takes about three months to complete a twelve-thousand-word work for the publisher, but I only write for digital publication part-time.

As far as disposing of used books, I part with very few since most contain my sticky notes, observations, and cross-references, and I occasionally revisit them. But I have donated books to hospitals and libraries, and given them to anyone willing to pick them up when I advertise their availability. They have already paid for themselves ten times over.

> *If you find yourself reading a book that appears to not offer anything new, it still might have value if it clarifies ideas that are complicated or confusing. My suggestion to you is to bear in mind you must offer something different or new that your readers are unlikely to have heard about. For example, I recently submitted a book to Bookboon that challenges a common belief that you should never check email in the morning. Its title is self-explanatory:* Always Check Email in the Morning and Other Brain-Based Strategies. *It explains what happens in your brain if you leave email unchecked while you try to write or do other work, and how this wastes time and reduces your productivity.*
>
> *When I read a book, I feel that if I get one new idea that could help me in any way, the book has more than paid for itself. The benefits continue well into the future. You can tell which books I enjoyed or disliked by the amount of highlighting and comments scribbled on their pages.*

> *I seldom read a nonfiction book in its entirety. I am only interested in specific information and topics, but other chapters could be of interest later.*

Patricia Westerhof, in her book *The Canadian Guide to Creative Writing & Publishing*, says that writers read differently from other people. And this is certainly true in my case. I read books in my genre to discover what has already been covered on the topic I have chosen to write on, and more importantly, what has *not* been covered. I also read nonfiction books on other topics that could be relevant to my topic. For example, what recent findings in psychology, neurology, neuroplasticity and so on could be applied to time management, leadership, or whatever topic I am writing about at the time.

I always read books on the topic I plan to write on next. For a book discussing the need for different time management strategies for today's digital age of speed, I revisited several books from my library on how the brain works, and several other books, including Oliver Burkeman's *Four Thousand Weeks* (2023), Johann Hari's *Stolen Focus* (2023), and Gloria Mark's *Attention Span* (2023). I am also planning to write a book on the power of patience in leadership, so I purchased several books on patience as well as several others that have at least a chapter on the topic. I will highlight text and make notes on many of the pages, either agreeing or disagreeing with the author, and indicating examples from my experience. This will help me get quickly into the topic once I start.

Speaking of Books ...

I believe in reading books by other authors who share ideas for writing effectively. I have listed several in the bibliography at the end of this book. One I enjoyed reading was Jami Attenberg's book *1000 Words: A Writer's Guide to Staying Creative, Focused, and Productive All Year Round* (2024). It includes comments from fifty other successful writers based on their experiences. Here are a few examples of the suggestions or comments that these authors shared, merged with a few of my own.

Will Leitch, the author of at least six books and a contributing editor at *New York* magazine, claims the hardest part of writing is getting it down in the first place. He says you can always fix your work later. He sees writing as making something that didn't exist before. In other words, you can't work with something if it's only in your head. You need something tangible to work on, so don't worry about the quality—just put it down on paper or onto your computer.

Elizabeth McCracken, author of several novels, says writers love to give advice about writing because they enjoy talking to themselves. I see that as my problem. I don't always practice what I preach, so I make it a point to review what I have already written on writing, which currently consists of three eBooks besides this book, and several articles. I make sure I take my own advice, but full disclosure—my advice doesn't even work for me all the time. So don't feel you have to force yourself to do something that just doesn't seem to fit your style.

For example, Maurice Ruffin, author of *The Ones Who Don't Say They Love You*, and others, gives me permission to sometimes scrap what I've written. I'm a packrat when it comes to saving copy that even editing can't save. I have been telling writers to keep unused material in a document on their computer. That's okay if you think it will fit somewhere else, but if you start over because it just wasn't how you wanted to say something, it's okay to scrap it. He says he tends to write the new piece two or three times faster than the original. I've done this with a full chapter in this book, and Ruffin is right.

Dirtbag Massachusetts, written by Isaac Fitzgerald, a *New York Times* bestselling author, reminds me of how I maintained my output of articles when I needed a weekly article for my blog, one for a biweekly column, and another for a monthly newsletter. My morning routine was different then. I used to walk to a distant coffee shop and develop an article outline in my mind as I walked. I was always able to think more clearly when walking, and by the time I reached the coffee shop, I had an idea of what I was going to write. It took me a full forty-five minutes or more of writing to get it down on paper while I had my coffee. I then walked to my office and did the necessary editing and dictated the result using voice-activated software. I have since changed my morning routine.

Fitzgerald has his coffee before he leaves on his walk, and says he is a better thinker when he moves as opposed to sitting still. He carries a notebook in his back pocket and sits down on a park bench or a grassy knoll, or takes a seat in a restaurant to put words on paper. He also writes longhand. He says that staring at a blank computer screen that's to be filled with words can be overwhelming. But he tends to correct every mistake or typo as he goes along, slowing down the process. Simply getting a first draft on paper frees him from this tendency.

Jami Attenberg's other forty-five contributing writers also make interesting comments. I love how Jami expresses the way she makes use of idle moments like being trapped in a doctor's waiting room or in the window seat during a three-hour flight. She refers to it as "filling the holes in your schedule." I have a lot of holes in my schedule, so I make sure I have writing materials with me, including a book or two, whenever I'm away from my office.

I have adopted several ideas from books on writing, including the suggestion to be patient, persistent, and prayerful, get plenty of sleep, and avoid the Bermuda Triangle of writing, which is usually between one and three in the afternoon. I now practice all five.

I'm not sure if this next idea was original or if it came from a book. I used it back in 1980. If writing a book seems overwhelming, and your genre is nonfiction, try doing what I did when I wrote my first book. Write articles on your chosen topic in a logical order and later piece them together to form a book. Almost anyone can write one article a week. You don't even need to have them published first. That first book of mine was probably not very good from a professional writer's perspective, but thanks to an aggressive promotion department within the publishing company, it did well.

I gave my speaking itinerary to the publisher and they arranged interviews with TV, radio, and newspapers as I traveled throughout the U.S. and Canada fulfilling my time management speaking engagements. And the experience also paved the way to have my next three books published by the same original publisher. Not bad for a novice part-time writer.

Good things can happen if you keep reading and writing—and persevering.

Chapter 5

Solving Writer's Block

Some writers never experience writer's block. Others spend more time staring at a blank computer screen or an empty note pad than they spend writing. What some people call writer's block is frequently a lack of planning. Past studies have shown that professional writers spend 40 percent of their time planning, 25 percent writing, and 35 percent editing. That is probably close to what I do now. But I used to spend about 10 percent of my time planning, 80 percent of my time writing, and the last 10 percent editing. Planning for me now includes that time reading other books and materials, deciding what to include in each chapter, outlining the book by writing chapter headings, and so on. Many authors say that success is in editing. Editing is extremely important, but the more planning you do, the less editing is necessary.

If you know the John Grisham formula, which is knowing what you want to say before you start, there is less chance that you will have writer's block. Grisham, who has had almost fifty consecutive number-one bestsellers, suggests you don't write the first scene until you know the final scene. If you know the final scene, it's hard to get lost.

Other fiction authors at one of our writers' groups have told me they know where they are heading because they have the story they want to write already in their minds, and so they deal with the details as they write the narrative. There seems to be no hard and fast rules. But I would assume the more planning you do, the less exposed you will be to the onset of writer's block.

A fellow part-time writer, Laura Leist, author of the book *Chaos at Work: 25 Techniques to Increase Productivity*, probably doesn't suffer from writer's block because she's a firm believer in planning. She maps out a table of contents and assigns time frames and due dates for each chapter. She also blocks out time in her calendar each week to do the actual writing.

Having an outline of each chapter before you start, as Laura Leist suggests, is a good idea. I also have folders for both hard copy and digital materials that are identified by topic (for example, all the management topics I might write about in the future). They currently number over one hundred manila folders and perhaps half that number of digital documents. In those folders I accumulate any relevant information that I come across related to those topics. Ideas, quotes, research items, articles (whether I had written them or not), and even notes to myself, go into those folders. I will explain my writing process in more detail in the next chapter.

Tips to Avoid Writer's Block

Ted Schwarz, author of the book *Time Management for Writers* claims, that 99.9 percent of writer's block is caused by boredom. He says this because of the nature of a writer's job—focusing on the same activity every day—that of writing. But this doesn't necessarily apply to part-time writers since they seldom have an opportunity to work all day writing. And it's hard to get bored when you write for only ninety minutes at a time and if you love writing.

I believe, however, that as a nonfiction writer, a change is as good as a rest, and I agree with switching to another topic (as recommended by Schwarz as well) but only if you experience a dry spell where you don't know what to do next. I have two or three books on the go most times and would not hesitate to give my brain a rest if this ever happened. I could always switch to another one if I hit a wall on the primary book.

The books I am working on are usually quite different from one another, which would help as well if I made the switch. One is an eBook, one is a book to be self-published, and if there's a third one, it's one I am writing for submission to a publishing house. That's the situation now, as I write this book. If this one is not accepted for publication, or I change my mind, I will either create a few eBooks out of it or break it into articles for my blog, or self-publish it. It's hard to fail when you have options.

L. Perry Wilbur and Jon Samsel, in their book *How to Write Articles that Sell*, also agree that one advantage of having more than one project running at the same time is that if you get stuck on one, you can turn to another one. But the reason I have two or three books on the go is not to avoid boredom or because I come to a standstill, but to be able to capture thoughts on those other topics if they pop into my mind as I write. Sometimes I think something that I am about to write or have already written would be a better fit in one of the other books. But I am only focused on one book at a time; otherwise, it would be multitasking, complete with all its negative effects on productivity.

But selecting two or more topics to write about next is being proactive, which is a form of planning. I doubt this would work well with fiction, however. I'd probably get my characters and story lines mixed up. I find nonfiction much easier to write.

> ***Writing Fiction vs. Nonfiction***
>
> *With nonfiction, I find that if you know what you are writing about and have plenty of information to give to your readers, you will never experience writer's block. Once you have provided all the information you have on hand, the book may be shorter than expected, but complete. I suppose that's true with fiction as well. John Grisham's book,* Camino Island, *is only 136,000 words long (okay, it's longish, but not quite Charles Dickens). With nonfiction you don't have to entertain your readers. You must educate them. But a little humor and entertainment frequently makes the chore of learning a little easier for them*

Writer's Block or Procrastination?

Despite what I think, most writers report having writer's block at one time or another, if you include procrastination and brain fog as well. And sometimes it's difficult to know the difference. It may simply be a case of procrastination, which is simply putting off things that you have decided to do. Most people procrastinate occasionally. Weak task initiation is one of the major causes of poor time management. Piers Steel, a University of Calgary psychologist, after analyzing psychological literature, concluded that 95 percent of people admit that they sometimes procrastinate.

It might help if you tell other people about your goals and intentions. That's one advantage of joining a writers' group. Make commitments to write at scheduled times by blocking off time in your planning calendar. To-do lists are just intentions, while scheduled blocks of time are commitments. Predetermined starting times, including those ninety-minute blocks of time in which to do your writing, is a basic time management principle.

Deadlines Help

Earlier I mentioned Laura Leist, who is a stickler for deadlines. Ted Schwarz, who wrote a book, *Time Management for Writers*, back in 1988, also believed in setting deadlines. He added the caveat that when you do this, allow time for problems that could arise along the way. Deadlines and priorities go hand in hand.

Deadlines are frequently motivational. Daniel H. Pink, in his book *When: The Scientific Secrets of Perfect Timing*, gave the example of Kiva, a non-profit organization that offers low-interest loans. The people at Kiva found that many applicants failed to complete a lengthy online application, but 24 percent more applicants did complete it when they were assigned a specific deadline for completion. Pink also gave the example that a gift certificate valid for only two weeks is three times more likely to be redeemed than the same one valid for two months.

Deadlines, when applied to writing projects, give you something to work towards and are better than simply writing when you get the urge. But my goal is to write for at least ninety minutes every morning. It has become a habit, and over the last eleven years has resulted in an average of four eBooks a year and one self-published every two years, which is fine with me. And as I mentioned, I don't recall ever experiencing writer's block. Not yet anyway. It could still happen. But writing articles, newsletters, and devotionals at other times seems to prime the pump. The best cure for writer's block is to keep writing.

A word of caution: deadlines and due dates that are far away seldom register in one's mind. You must flip pages in a planning calendar to see the reminder. That's one reason I prefer to use a week-at-a-glance planner rather than just a-day-at-a-glance. And I make it a habit every Monday morning to flip a few pages ahead to view my plans and commitments.

Tame the Stress in Your Life

If you are under stress or anxious or worried for any reason, you will be more vulnerable to writer's block. You may find it difficult to concentrate or be creative. The authors of *Neuroscience for Leadership* say, "The experience of stress, sustained over long periods of time can have a powerful and widespread negative impact on your thinking, feeling, health and productivity." This applies to any work or job, not just writing.

As the authors of the above book claim, stress is unavoidable. It comes with this digital age of speed, but we can dissipate it and continue to live with it by building resilience. Writing is an excellent way of coping with stress. Most books will recommend exercising such things as journaling to release you from its negative effects. Handwriting is even better from a health standpoint. I may be exaggerating its impact, but as I describe in the conclusion, I found writing poetry to be therapeutic. Not for publication, but simply to expel the emotions inside me, whether that was grief, regret, worry, frustration, or whatever.

Exercise of any kind, whether jogging, swimming, walking, or simply standing up and moving around helps. Whenever I had an argument with my wife, I'd go for a walk. I jokingly used to accuse her of starting an argument just to get me out of the house. Even more important is sleep, and many writers get too little of it. I seldom skip afternoon naps, and when I do, I have one after dinner. It makes up for my frequent late nights watching sporting events on TV. (I do realize that watching people exercise doesn't count as a stress reliever.)

Jordan Rosenfeld, in her chapter on blocks to the creative flow in the Writer's Digest book *The Complete Handbook of Novel Writing*, prefers to call it "inertia" as opposed to writer's block. But the remedies are similar either way, including word count goals, accountability, exercise, and so on. Writer's block is a mind thing. The body and mind are part of the same system. One impacts the other. Just as background music, positive attitude, and a "count your blessings" attitude all help prevent writer's block, so do the physical activities mentioned as well. Do what works best for you.

Chapter 6

The Writing Process

Because I write nonfiction, I have been collecting information on various business topics for over forty years. It is interesting how many recommendations from decades ago are no longer viable today. Strategies such as cutting down on sleep, multitasking, using the Pomodoro technique, not checking email in the morning, thinking it takes twenty-one days to form a habit (or any special time frame), are no longer recommended. My latest eBook, *Always Check Email in the Morning and Other Brain-Based Strategies*, discusses many of these strategies that no longer apply. For writers, strategies that become obsolete permit them to introduce something new to their readers.

Whenever I think of a topic to write about, I label both an electronic and manila folder and start accumulating relevant information on that topic. Once I have decided on the topic I will write about next, I make up additional folders for chapter headings based on what I think should be covered in the book and separate the material into those corresponding folders. The material in each folder gives me ideas on what should be included. In addition to research, my experience as a manager for twelve years, a business teacher for eight years, and an owner of companies is rich fodder for topics. (If you write nonfiction, you should always write on topics you know something about.)

I number the chapter folders in an order that makes sense. I can always change that later. I also buy the latest books on the chapter topics. That might be another reason I don't experience writer's block. (If you don't highlight or make notes in your books you can save money by using library books where possible.) Those books and those folders are on my desk as I write.

Most of my publications present my views on management and leadership topics, and most of these are the important, but often overlooked, soft skills such as trust, proactivity, character, patience, attitude, and so on. For eight thousand to twelve-thousand-word publications, I have no trouble delivering enough information on topics of interest to readers, and hopefully they all add value to what's already out there. I no longer need books to further my career in speaking since I am no longer on the speaking circuit.

How could I possibly experience writer's block when I'm surrounded by books and other materials related to my topic? I have hundreds of articles that I have written in the past (most of them on the same topic as my books). Yes, I keep them in both digital (easy to cut and paste) and in hard copy format. They go back to 40 BC (Before Computers). They are from my blog articles, columns, devotionals, newsletters, and the magazines that I used to publish decades ago. I am a literary packrat.

When you file anything, be sure to include the date and source. For instance, "*Toronto Star*, July 30, 2024." It's a lot more difficult to track down the source two or three years later. And some publications insist that you include the source for anything that is not original. When I start to write a book, I usually begin with the chapter that has the most information in its folder. With nonfiction, chapters don't have to be in the right order when you first write them. I view the initial writing of the manuscript as part of the planning process. Sometimes I write the introduction first, and sometimes I don't.

Write Fast and Edit Slow

Full disclosure: I got this heading from the contents page of Paula LaRocque's *The Book on Writing: The Ultimate Guide to Writing Well.* When you write fast, you tend to avoid inserting unnecessary adjectives and adverbs, keep sentences short, and allow fewer pauses, let alone stopping, so you have less chance of suffering from writer's block. When you edit your work, you normally take out everything that doesn't directly impact the story that you're telling or the information you are providing. And you can "add it in" as well as "edit it out" if you think a word looks naked without a little dressing.

Don't stop writing to proofread or edit until you have finished writing for the day. Maintain the momentum once you start. Scheduling short sessions of ninety minutes or less at a time usually results in fewer delays. As I've pointed out, few people can retain a high level of concentration for more than ninety minutes without a break. This could change once you are engrossed in your work but most of us have jobs besides writing and cannot afford longer writing sessions anyway. As I mentioned previously, the one ninety-minute session every morning is frequently all the writing I do for the day, yet I always manage to stay on target for producing four books a year. I only wish that publishers could keep pace, because they seem to take longer to publish than they did in the past.

In Paula LaRocque's book, she tells of author Ann Lamott in a radio interview saying there was a time she couldn't write if there were dishes in the sink, but now she could write if there was a corpse in the sink. The more you write the easier it is to focus.

Editing Tips

Stuck for a word? Place a few dashes and keep going. Chances are when you read it later the right word will pop into your mind. The opening scene of any book, whether fiction or nonfiction, should move along quickly. And of course, be interesting. Take two pages to describe how someone got lost and you may lose the reader as well.

Keeping sentences short speeds up reading. One main idea is all that a sentence can handle, so don't embarrass it by giving it too many words to juggle. Get right to the point and stay there.

According to Dimitriadis and Psychogios, in their book *Neuroscience for Leaders*, the brain expends almost 90 percent of its energy on our body's functions to ensure our survival. It doesn't have much left for the thinking required for writing books, especially after exhausting most of this residual amount on our full-time jobs—assuming we are only writing part-time. This means we can't waste energy by forcing ourselves to burn the midnight oil or engage in marathon writing sessions. Doing so will deplete our energy to the extent that we not only have writer's block but might be putting our health at risk as well.

Another evil is multitasking. Switching back and forth between several books and other jobs puts pressure on our working memory and increases the cognitive load on our brain. It also depletes our energy.

I assume that writers who take advantage of their prime time, like John Grisham who writes in the mornings only, never experience writer's block nor would they suffer from energy depletion.

I would wager that those few famous writers who write from dawn to dusk and become the most prolific writers of all time also might be the ones with health problems or have shorter lifespans.

I'm reminded of the fable of the tortoise and the hare. The hare was certainly a much faster runner, but those down times lost the race for him. Similarly, the writer's goal should not be to work long and hard when they have large chunks of time available, such as weekends or evenings, but to work in shorter but steadier chunks of time on a regular daily basis. It conserves energy. Your prime time for writing, based on your chronotype, can be either morning or night, but not both.

If you come to a standstill, switch to another writing project for a half-hour or more as already mentioned, or take a brief walk around your desk and do a few stretches. If you just can't get started again, write anything to quick-start the flow again. Once you start writing, the creative juices will flow, and you can edit out any superfluous material later. Don't wait for creativity to reveal itself. If you stare at the computer screen, it will simply stare back at you. The best way to avoid writer's block is to keep writing.

When your time is up for each writing session and you must stop, write one more sentence but don't finish it, except in your head. Reading that partial sentence and finishing it at the next session will help pick up your train of thought and build momentum faster than starting from scratch. Some writers have more trouble starting than continuing.

In Praise of Cursive Writing

Virginia Ann Byrd, in her book *Still Writing*, also recommends that initially you just start writing. It doesn't even have to relate to your topic. She also suggests you write longhand with pen and paper. She doesn't say why, but it is easier to write in longhand because most of us started in grade school with pencil and paper, not with typewriters or laptops. And cursive writing is a brain health activity, so you gain that as well.

One post in *Psychology Today* claims, "Handwriting stimulates complex brain connections essential in encoding new information and forming memories." I know from experience that if I write a lot—in diaries, time planners, grocery lists, etc.—I'm more likely to retain the information and recall it later. And according to the article mentioned above, it improves the speed of recall by as much as 25 percent.

Cursive writing stimulates the parts of the brain that control critical thinking, memory, and language, three things that are critical for a career in writing. The brain doesn't learn as efficiently when typing.

Neurologists in general recommend exercising the brain as well as the body, and although some people claim that handwriting is outdated and behind the times, this is only true if you feel it's outdated to have a healthy brain. As mentioned in a *New York Times* article, putting pen to paper stimulates the brain like nothing else. And there is no denying its positive impact on working memory and long-term memory alike.

There are many well-known writers who wrote longhand. A thirty-nine-year-old housewife in Indiana always dreamed of writing a novel, and finally did so by writing at a card table when her kids were at school. Her novel, *The Man Who Loved Cat Dancing*, became a bestseller and was adapted for a motion picture. The author, Marilyn Durham, followed up with another bestseller called *Dutch Uncle* the following year. Arthur Hailey, author of such books as *Airport, Wheels, Hotel, The Money Changers* and others, wrote the first draft of his novels in longhand, paragraph by paragraph.

I write all my books longhand first and then dictate each day's work to my laptop using Microsoft's voice-activated software. I also do a lot of cutting and pasting as I use information from my blog articles, newsletters, devotionals, and old columns that I had written in the past. Frequently you can reuse past material if you still retain the rights, and it's directed at a different market.

The Power of Persistence

Regina Brett, in her book *God Never Blinks*, says to write piece by piece, completing one project at a time. "Finish one short story. One poem. Make a commitment to finish things." I did start with one short story followed by others, but never sold any. I then completed a poem, followed by other poems. Then I tried several anecdotes. Greeting card ideas. Nonfiction articles. And, eventually, a nonfiction book. The book succeeded in finding a publisher.

I was impatient, lacked persistence, and used up my energy trying to be published instead of trying to be good at what I wanted to do. That's what Anne Lamott said in her book *Bird by Bird: Some Instructions on Writing and Life.* "The problem that comes up over and over again is that these people want to be published. They kind of want to write but what they really want is to be published."

Lamott hit the nail on the head with her assessment. Getting published will not make you a good writer. That becomes obvious in today's writing world of self-publishing, on-demand printing, and vanity presses.

Anyone can be published if that's the goal. You could probably save enough money to do that much faster than learning to write well.

Is there anything wrong with self-publishing or paying companies to publish your book? Of course not. It's a publishing solution many authors use. You can make money if you are good at marketing, or you pay others who are good at marketing, but it doesn't prove you're good at writing. If sales are great, it may only prove you're good at marketing, or someone you hire is good at marketing.

Your book is just another product to sell. As a time management consultant and a speaker, I also sold products that helped people to manage their time. I started out selling other people's products—planning calendars, telephone directories, checklists, and so on. I made money selling them, but the money was only a measure of our success at selling.

Chapter 7

Oh no, Not Another Rejection!

If you write a book and submit it without success to publishers, don't get discouraged. Be persistent. Jack Canfield and Mark Victor Hansen took their *Chicken Soup for the Soul* to over one hundred publishers. At the American Booksellers Association, Canfield and Hansen struck out again with numerous houses. Finally, a small publisher from Florida called Health Communication Inc. took a chance on the book. Even then, the authors didn't get an advance. The rest is history. I'm not suggesting you submit your manuscript to hundreds of publishers, but a few rejections do not mean your work is not publishable. Editors make mistakes. If your manuscript is rejected, you're in good company.

Sam Sinclair Baker had his *Scarsdale Diet* rejected by seventeen publishers. J.K. Rowling's first Harry Potter book was rejected a dozen times before it was published, and the publisher only printed one thousand copies. What does that tell you? And Stephen King had three novels rejected before Doubleday bought *Carrie*. That novel had been rejected thirty times before it was accepted. (Incidentally, I recommend you read Stephen King's *On Writing: A Memoir of the Craft* for his perspective on writing.)

At least five London-based publishers rejected Yann Martel's *Life of Pi*, but when it was finally accepted by Knopf, Canada, it sold over 10 million copies and later became an Academy Award-winning movie.

The examples of rejections received by successful authors far exceed the number of successful authors. Linda Sivertsen, in her book *Beautiful Writers*, says that Seth Godin, one of my favorite nonfiction authors, sent queries for hundreds of book ideas in one year to publishers and never received an offer. And Steven Pressfield wrote for seventeen years without selling anything.

Among the older, well-known books initially rejected are *Little Women*, *The Rise & Fall of the Third Reich*, *The Diary of Anne Frank* and *Kon Tiki*. As I said, if you have received rejection slips, you're among good company, such as Pearl Buck, George Orwell, and Dr. Seuss. J.K. Rowling's Harry Potter titles have sold more than 400 million copies, and yes, even Stephen King, John Grisham, and almost every other best-selling author have been rejected before making their fortunes in royalty payments.

One writer took rejections in stride by remarking that he never had to buy paper. He used the blank sides of rejection letters to draft his novels. Some publishers receive more than four thousand query letters and manuscripts every week. So you can't blame them for letting a few potential bestsellers slip through the cracks. Persistence is the key to success for most good writers.

Rejections Slips Are the Battle Scars of Writers

I think I would have been more successful in my writing career if I hadn't had the grandiose idea of submitting material to the top paying publications such as *Reader's Digest*, *Saturday Evening Post*, and *Chatelaine*. Few things are more responsible for taking the wind out of your sails. In my teen years I accepted only my mother's biased assessment, and that kept me going.

I think being able to accept rejection and criticism is an important factor in becoming a successful writer. As I mentioned, one magazine editor suggested I start writing fiction articles when I had something to say, which is to say to experience life before I started writing about it.

He was right for more reasons than he realized. As a youngster I was too young to process rejections successfully. The reasoning part of my brain, the prefrontal cortex which houses the "executive function," takes about twenty years to fully develop. As a result, I associated rejection with failure rather than with learning. So I sulked and stopped writing for months, ignoring the fact that a few of the editors had even offered suggestions, and a couple said they would take a second look if I made some changes. But I was too wrapped up in my ego to even consider that.

Eventually I started anew, taking the path of least resistance. I abandoned my dream of being a storyteller, and instead submitted fillers in the form of anecdotes, short verse, epigrams, and whatever I noticed was being used in various magazines. I wasn't much of a philosopher in those days, but at least I had a sense of humor and some knowledge of what teenagers and college students went through. I still recall a few of my earlier submissions to lesser known publications such as *The Link*, *American Legion Magazine*, and *Quote*. For example, two of the verses

I recall getting published are "The needs of a student at college are known. Pay him a visit but leave them a loan." And, "With socks at my ankles I find myself thinking my mom has the power of positive shrinking."

When they started being accepted, I learned another lesson. Rejection may seem demotivating and demoralizing, but the first acceptance is motivational and exhilarating. It put me in a more positive frame of mind, and there was no holding me back. Rejected pieces rolled harmlessly onto the revision pile like beads of water off a duck's back. And to prevent rejections from dampening my hope of a sale, I always had two or three more submissions in the mail before the answers came back on the previous ones. That's the beauty of writing fillers such as epigrams, poems, short verse, and greeting card ideas. They don't take much writing time compared to articles, novellas, or books. Even with books you can send out simultaneous submissions to different publishers, but let them know you are doing that.

Learn from Rejections

I learned another lesson from the editors of *MacLean's* magazine. *MacLean's* started up long before I was born, in 1905. Much later, during the Depression in the 1930s, the magazine added a new section called "Parade." It was meant "to cheer up the people with a little levity," according to Suzy Aston and Sue Ferguson in their article, "MacLean's: The First 100 Years." As outlined in the article, it was "a feature that contained a potpourri of humorous slices of life from across the country."

That was right up my alley, and I submitted very brief stories of humorous happenings, which happened to be mostly about my father. I made a small fortune (hundreds of dollars in total in those days) talking about him, such as answering the door on Halloween with a hammer from a picture-hanging event still in his hand, and the little goblins scattering in all directions. And the time the stovepipes caught on fire back in the 1940s because creosote had accumulated and ignited. Mom ran out of the house screaming for Dad, who was picking apples in our tiny orchard. "The house is on fire! The house is on fire!" she yelled. Possessing the exact opposite personality of my Type A mother, my dad walked quickly to the house, reached into his pocket for his tobacco and papers, and rolled a cigarette as he observed the red-hot pipes. Saying nothing, he simply hooked a kitchen chair in place with his left foot, climbed on the chair, and calmly lit his cigarette on the pipe. We all knew he was in control of the situation.

I agree neither scenario was that funny, but the editor of that department, with a few deft changes, made the stories hilarious. My lesson? Don't ignore the recommendations of an editor who sees hundreds of submissions a month. I had been too busy bemoaning my fate to pay attention to what the editor was saying about my short stories. Success is often in editing.

I have never heard of a successful writer who has never been rejected. Stephen King, in his book, *On Writing*, tells of his first story being rejected with a form letter criticizing his decision to use a staple instead of a paper clip. Did he rant and rave and retire from writing? No. Next time he used a paper clip.

I learned to edit and re-edit, submit and resubmit, study the target publication for the type of fillers they use, and my sales increased. When I attacked the greeting card market, I targeted companies that published studio cards because my offerings were meant to make the reader smile. Rejections didn't bother me because I had over a dozen more card companies on my list who might accept them, and frequently they did.

By the time I was able to do some serious nonfiction writing, I had the resilience necessary to accept rejection for what it is—a fact of life. And perhaps those "Sorry, your submission does not meet our current editorial requirements" replies could very well be true. I understand that these days it could take three months or more to even hear back from some publishers. And in many cases, you never hear back from them. That's what's referred to as a silent rejection.

Chapter 8

Editing Your Manuscript

You might want to hire someone to edit your work. If you do, use an experienced editor who will be unbiased and unafraid to suggest changes. You can get a list of editors at Editors Canada (**https://editors.ca**). You can also get free information there on what to expect from a professional editor. And there are similar associations in the U.S. and Canada.

Or refer to Jeff Herman's *Guide to Book Publishers, Editors and Literary Agents, 2023.* It also has useful information on self-publishing, query letters, publishers, proposals, agents, and so on. It is a valuable resource for serious writers. You can order a copy through your local bookstore or at Amazon, and your local library might have a copy.

Personally, I prefer to work with an editor I have worked with before or who has come highly recommended. In 1980 I met Don Loney, an editor with General Publishing in Toronto, Canada. (Don edited this book. Please don't do the math about our ages.) He has come a long way since then and has worked at several major publishers such as McGraw Hill Canada, HarperCollins, and John Wiley & Sons. He now freelances and primarily works with small houses.

Editors frequently have a minimum fee that they charge, so make sure you get a quote before committing. I belong to the Word Guild in Canada, which is an association of writers and editors who are Christian. In the past I hired a freelance editor to edit notes I had made up for a new time management course I had developed. It was forty-eight pages in length and ran to twelve thousand words. The editor looked at the project and then gave me a cost so there were no surprises—and it was reasonable.

Whether you are looking for an editor, distributor, agent, or publishing house, it's a good idea to ask for recommendations from those who have already had books published. Most people would be happy to help you out. That's another advantage of joining a writer's group.

Amanda Lang, in *The Power of Why*, says that outsiders have a big advantage when it comes to innovative thinking because they have more psychological distance from the situation at hand. She is not talking about writing per se when she says this, but I can see the application. Perhaps that's another reason to distance yourself from your manuscript at the editing stage, either by leaving it alone for several weeks or farming out the editing task to someone else.

Editing, Like Cheese, Improves with Aging

The editing process, like wine or cheese, improves with aging. Until recently, I edited all my books myself. It is difficult to edit your own work, but if you do, let the book marinate for a few weeks. If you're not pressed for time, you might make the aging process even longer. You tend to see what you think you wrote, and not what has been written.

One author, Zadia Smith, who was quoted by Virginia Ann Byrd in her book *I'm Still Writing*, suggests you put your manuscript in a drawer for as long as you can, even if it's a year or more. She says, "The secret to editing your book is to become its reader instead of its writer." I have never left a manuscript unattended for longer than two weeks, but I can see the wisdom in that statement.

As Zadie Smith mentions, it's not the head of a writer you need to edit your work. And not even the head of a professional editor. It's the head of a stranger who picks up the book and begins to read it. It is easier to spot other people's mistakes than your own. What her advice means is that you should not be afraid to cut out any parts that do not relate to the purpose of the book. When you edit out large chunks of copy, keep them in a folder on your computer for possible use in future works.

I find it's easier to edit when you read the manuscript aloud. If you stumble over a phrase, or anything is ambiguous or sounds awkward, editing is in order. Change anything that doesn't read smoothly or is unclear. Paula LaRocque also says that reading aloud ought to be an integral part of the editing process.

If you are doing your own editing, it's also a good idea to enlist the help of readers who represent the market segment for your book. This can be done long before you finish the manuscript so you can easily incorporate any changes or suggested additions.

You could assign a chapter or two to each person, so they are not overwhelmed. Offer them a free copy of your book once it is published. Don't feel obligated to incorporate all the suggestions, but be receptive to suggestions. Don't be on the defensive.

If you're writing in a technical or specialized area, you might want to form a panel of experts from that area to critique your manuscript and offer suggestions. When I was writing a book on time management for school principals, the New Jersey publishing company formed a committee of volunteer principals to review my work, offer suggestions, and help tailor the material to their profession and work environment.

As you edit, keep in mind that magazines or other publications may want to take excerpts from your book. You could make your material easy to use for this purpose by including discrete sections such as 10 Ways to Stop Procrastinating or 5 Steps to a More Organized Life. They could be used as separate sidebars or integrated into the chapters. You could also use them for promotional flyers, articles, or items in your newsletter. This is a case of being marketing minded, even during the writing and editing process.

Subtractive Sculpting Applied to Writing

Michelangelo was a subtractive sculptor. He used a mallet and chisels and other tools to free a figure he visualized in a block of marble. It is the oldest form of sculpture. Many artists can visualize the finished piece of art in that block of granite or wood or ice or whatever medium they are using, and free it by chipping away any unwanted parts. They must be careful not to chip away too much, however, or they risk spoiling the sculpture.

Sometimes writers are quick to edit and impatient to publish. Careful editing is extremely important. At the Academy Awards, in about two-thirds of the cases, the movie nominated for "Best Film Editing" has gone on to win "Best Picture." And the editing of a book manuscript can make the difference between a publishing contract and a rejection slip.

There could be a best-selling book in your finished manuscript, but you must chip away anything that only serves to obscure the main purpose of that book.

Editing usually refers to preparing written material for publication by correcting, condensing, or otherwise modifying it. For example, Stephen King describes his experience as a teenager when submitting a report on a basketball game in his book *On Writing*. His piece was completely transformed by an editor. The editor did it by deleting unnecessary words. After the edit, he told King, "When you write a story, you are telling yourself the story. When you rewrite, your main job is taking out all the things that are not the story."

Similarly, when you are working on any job, you should eliminate everything that is not the job. This might include unnecessary tasks and activities, as well as interruptions and distractions. Most people can increase their personal productivity and relieve stress in the process simply by editing out any work that does not help achieve their goals.

As Gary Keller said in his book *The One Thing: The Surprisingly Simple Truth behind Extraordinary Results*, "Don't focus on being busy; focus on being productive." To do this, you must focus on those tasks and activities that contribute most to the achievement of your goals. Busy work, distractions, interruptions, and so on must be edited out of your day.

The similarity between editing a piece of writing and editing a piece of your day ends here. It takes more than a stroke of a pen to delete interruptions for instance. But with self-discipline, and a set of personal policies that include when and how often you will check your email, silence your smartphone, visit social media, and so on, you can edit out a lot of nonproductive time.

If you run a business, you can also edit out unprofitable products as well as unnecessary activities that consume valuable time. For example, I used to write a weekly blog article for my website and post it on social media. Recently, I reduced this activity to every second week, and I am considering reducing it even more. I am sure it will have little or no impact on my business. But it will help relieve the stress of my self-imposed deadlines, and free up time for more important activities, such as my paid writing projects. The original purpose of these articles was to force me to keep writing, since most of the material could then be used in my books. Today, I no longer need that incentive to write.

Whether you want to become a prolific writer, a more profitable business, or a more peaceful person, you must visualize the kind of day you want to have and edit out anything you see that is not part of that day. Become a subtractive sculptor.

I would suggest that the second most important activity for authors and writers is editing. The most important activity of course, is to keep writing, so that when it comes time to edit, a complete draft is ready for that process.

Whether you write books, articles, fiction, nonfiction, essays, or whatever, you use words to do it. And the words you use and how you use them determine the success of your work. So don't skip the next chapter, even though it's wordy.

Chapter 9

Write with Your Reader in Mind

I recall as a child being encouraged by my mother to study "Word Power" in the *Reader's Digest* to improve my vocabulary. "If each week you were to learn to use one more word correctly in a sentence, by the time you graduate from high school ..." she admonished. I completed her sentence for her: "... nobody will understand what I'm saying."

I didn't know how prescient my silly remark was. I did build my vocabulary out of respect for, and to impress, my mother. Then I discovered that many magazines (and some of quality) paid by the word which created a perfect storm of rejections. It wasn't until the late 1950s or early 1960s that I learned the truth via a letter replacing the usual blunt rejection slip. The magazine editor, among other criticisms too humiliating to mention, said, "You are not writing for our reader; you are writing for yourself."

In other words, I sounded like a pompous ass with my three-syllable adjectives and adverbs and high-sounding phraseology that skyrocketed my writing to a fog index approaching university-level tomes. In actual fact, I had been writing not for myself or my reader, but for my mother. From that point on I started writing more like I speak, and to my surprise, started to see my name in print.

How to Keep Your Work Focused on Your Reader

Several years ago, I gave a basic course on effective writing. Here's basically what I shared in one of the handouts— some hints on effective writing—with apologies to both my late mother and *Reader's Digest*. I quote: Whether you are writing reports, articles or email messages, the same principles of effective writing apply. The objective is to communicate clearly and succinctly so the reader can grasp your meaning quickly without having to re-read a sentence or paragraph."

Below are some suggestions to liven up the writing and maintain your reader's interest. Avoid long, confusing sentences. Write in the active voice. Stay away from clichés. Don't be redundant. Don't convert verb forms to noun forms. And leave out unnecessary words.

Use the Active Voice

In the active voice, the subject of the sentence does the acting as opposed to the passive voice, where the subject is acted upon. For instance, the active voice is being used in the sentence "The president held a meeting," as opposed to the passive voice in "A meeting was held by the president." Using the active voice makes your writing come alive. It is economical, clarifies meaning, and makes the action move along faster. See how much clearer and crisper the sentences become when they are written in the active voice.

But sometimes using the passive voice is essential,

such as in mystery novels, where the author doesn't want to reveal who took what action, such as "The man had been shot twice in the back of the head." The passive voice is used to emphasize the action or the object acted upon. But if you want to draw attention to the doer, you should go with the active voice.

Don't Convert Verb Forms to Noun Forms

Verbs are exciting; nouns are boring. You can liven up the action and reduce the verbiage in the process if you make sure you don't disguise verbs as nouns. "He decided" is succinct and lively compared to "He made a decision." The goal is to limit the number of words we use, as long as meaning is not affected. It's the message in our efforts, not length, that is of value to the reader.

Watch for Redundancy

So many words in the English language mean the same thing or are so close in meaning that we have gotten into the habit of including them in pairs, such as *close* proximity, *basic* fundamentals and *end* result. The length of many messages can be reduced by a third or more simply by deleting all the needless repetition. For example, larger *in size* (how else could it be larger?) becomes simply "larger," and *regular* weekly meetings (as opposed to *irregular* weekly meetings?) becomes simply "weekly meetings.

Get Rid of Wordy Expressions

You can also reduce word clutter by avoiding wordy expressions that collectively form gobbledygook. Avoid clichés that simply add to the word count and frustrate the time-pressured reader who is interested in meaning, not words. Examples of clichés, those over-used, boring expressions that gives the impression that the writer is too lazy to have an original thought, include "Assuring you of our prompt attention ...", "In the not-too-distant future ...", and "It has come to my attention ..."

Substitute Shorter Words and Phrases for Unwieldly Ones

We don't want our book or article to read like a kindergarten book (unless we're writing to that age group.) But why use big words when small words will do? Smaller, simpler words are just as good as long, multi-syllabic words, and take less space, less time to write and read, and are less likely to be misunderstood. They move the action along faster, reduce word clutter and increase readability. For example, write "many" instead of "numerous" and "do" instead of "implement" and "rest" instead of "remainder."

Keep It Simple

Groups of words or expressions can often be simplified. This will help readability and reduce the danger of coming across as a pompous writer. Substitute "If" for "In the event of," and "Like" for "Along the lines of."

I believe Henry Malmgreen was his name—the editor who critiqued my writing, that is. We had no internet in those days, but I recently googled his name. He died in 1989, about thirty years after he sent me that letter. Any success I have had in improving my vocabulary, I owe to that man. And of course, my mother, who never stopped encouraging me—despite her love for big words.

Keep Communication Clear and Concise

It's the message in your writing, the story in your novel, and the information in your nonfiction article or book that is important to the reader. So make these elements as clear and concise as possible.

Here are a few more examples of how you can reduce verbiage. Instead of "He submitted his application by mail," say "He applied by mail." Replace "He gave an explanation for his actions," with "He explained his actions." And in place of "She issued payment for her membership fees," write "She paid her membership fees."

There are other ways to cut down on verbiage by replacing wordy expressions with a single word or two. For example:

"until such time as" > "until

"during the time that" >"while"

"in a satisfactory manner" >"satisfactorily"

"as of this date" > "to date"

"with the possible exception of" > "except for"

"the only other alternative" > "the alternative"

Ask yourself if the opposite of an adjective or adverb makes sense. If the answer is no, it's probably unnecessary. Don't use "considered opinion" if an "unconsidered opinion" wouldn't make sense. And don't use "practical experience" if "impractical experience" doesn't make sense. If you can eliminate a word without changing the meaning of a sentence, do so. The "more" in "more preferable" is redundant because preferable already means more desirable. In the same way, "very" in "very unique" is redundant because unique means one of a kind. You can't be more different than that!

Here are a few more examples of needless words and why they are superfluous:

My own personal feelings (as opposed to my own impersonal feelings?)

Free gift (are there gifts that are *not* free?)

With my own eyes (as opposed to someone else's

eyes?)

New recruit (as opposed to an old recruit?)

Potential hazard (don't all hazards carry risk?)

Stupid mistake (are there smart mistakes?)

Past experience (as opposed to experience that hasn't happened yet?)

Possible choices (as opposed to impossible choices?)

Rename it something else (as opposed to renaming it the same thing?)

Sworn affidavit (don't all affidavits have to be sworn?)

Past history (as opposed to future history?)

In two equal halves (is there such a thing as unequal halves?)

I was quite disappointed when I started writing for publication. The time spent increasing my vocabulary as a child was wasted as far as editors were concerned. One editor, when rejecting a short story that I had submitted, told me, "People don't talk like that."

So, if you happen to be writing for publication, rather than to impress, I will leave you with a few shorter equivalents for commonly used words:

function for functionality

many for numerous

person for individual

rest for remainder

first for initial

do for implement

enough for sufficient

try for attempt

effect for effectuate

use for utilization

end for terminate

so for accordingly

next for adjacent

get for acquire

show for demonstrate

clarify for elucidate

cut for incision.

Keep Your Writing Short, Simple, and Understandable

Take the example of someone setting a "new record" in pole sitting. I have never heard of a record that was *not* new. So trash the word "new." Similarly, a flight attendant tells us to "Take all your personal belongings with you when you deplane." Do you have belongings that are *not* personal? Would deleting the word "personal" confuse anyone?

Our daily conversations are overflowing with superfluous words, but you need not carry them into your writing. When you write, you can also edit. If the antonym of a word doesn't make sense, it's a safe bet you can delete it. So you don't need "conclusive" if "inconclusive proof" doesn't make sense. Or "desirable" if there is no such thing as "undesirable benefits." Or "good" if a "bad variety" doesn't make sense. Or "extremely" if you would never use "slightly ordinary." Or "regular" if there is no such thing as "irregular weekly meetings," and so on.

You could also be assured that all destinations are final, all choices are possible, all risks are calculated, and all requirements are mandatory, so you can delete the words in italics in the following expressions: *final* destination, *possible* choices, *calculated* risk, and *mandatory* requirement.

Of course the act of writing tempts us to use more words. Parkinson's Law seems to take hold and the number of words expands to fill the space available. So, we start off with "It has come to my attention …" or "In the not-too-distant future …" or "Please find attached …" Just say what you want to say.

Keep it simple. There are no points for pomposity or cash for complexity or victory in verbosity. Keeping written communication clear and concise is crucial. And remember that clarity takes priority over brevity. That's why I used both words, "clear" and "concise," when concise means both short and clear, or expressing what needs to be said without unnecessary words as according to the *Oxford Dictionary*, "giving a lot of information clearly and in a few words." If clarity requires a few more words, go for it.

Brevity Has a Limit

It seems that the tech world has latched onto only the brevity portion of conciseness and taken it to the nth degree. Instead of turning verbs into nouns, it has turned nouns into verbs. In emails, direct messages (DM), and social media platforms, we have Google (a search engine) as a verb that means "to search online." And a tweet, a sound originally uttered only by birds, is now a verb meaning "post a message on X (formerly Twitter)."

Acronyms have exploded into everyday correspondence such as LOL (Laughing out loud) and BRB (Be right back) and SMH (Shaking my head), and even less common ones, combined with emoticons (character combinations or pictorial symbols). A new dictionary may be required for us non-techie people so we can decipher communication.

In my day, we did have a few acronyms such as FYI (For your information), ASAP (As soon as possible), and KISS (Keep it simple, silly). But technology has helped take it to a new level.

I suppose our language is evolving with new words, changed meanings, cryptic phrases, acronyms, abbreviations, and informality all leading the way. But I hope everyday language isn't reduced to the point where I receive a closing text message saying, "CU, HT!" That's going a little too far.

If you want to explore further how the internet, mobile devices, and social media are changing the way we communicate, refer to Gretchen McCulloch's book *Because Internet: Understanding the New Rules of Language*. From prose to punctuation, changes are coming, and you may soon be able to see them in a dictionary near you.

Chapter 10

Recharge Your Brain
with Proper Sleep

Working long hours makes you good at one thing only—and that is working long hours. It does not increase your efficiency or effectiveness, which means as a writer your word output and quality will not improve just because you've made a greater effort. Lack of proper sleep will result in a slower pace, additional errors, frequent self-interruptions, susceptibility to distractions, and a decline in energy and motivation. Working long hours simply means your level of efficiency is stretched over a greater span of time. This is an example of Parkinson's Law, where work will expand to fill up the allotted time. About the only thing you will have to show for your dedication are sleepless nights, which cumulatively lead to sleep deprivation and a host of health issues.

Insufficient sleep slows both creative and logical thinking, as well as affecting motor skills and manual dexterity. Performance suffers as well as your health. Lack of sleep lowers the tolerance for frustration and heightens interpersonal sensitivity. It impairs focus, problem solving, and memory. We know that not getting enough sleep has been associated with reduced blood flow to the brain, which leads to bad decisions. But putting a heavy demand on the brain through continually working on cognitive tasks without sufficient breaks can have a similar effect. That's why you're more easily distracted when you are tired and have trouble remembering things.

Not only could working overtime interfere with sleep, but a study quoted in an article by Nicole Ostrow in the *Bloomberg News* concluded that adults working eleven hours a day or more had a 67 percent higher risk of developing heart disease than those who worked eight hours a day. Those who worked ten hours a day had a 45 percent higher risk of developing heart disease than those who worked eight hours a day. The study, reported in the *Annals of Internal Medicine*, followed 7,095 civil service workers in London, UK who were aged thirty-nine to sixty-two at the start of the trial. Their sleep habits, as well as their eating, exercising and stress levels are thought to be the factors that account for their risk for developing heart disease.

A separate study, which followed 2,123 British civil servants for six years, found that working long hours appeared to substantially increase a person's risk of becoming depressed. Employees who worked at least eleven hours a day had about two and a half times higher odds of developing depression than those who only worked seven or eight hours.

Energy management is required to maximize your performance, retain your health and protect your brain. This involves both gaining energy in the first place through such things as proper sleep, diet, and exercise, and managing the energy through judicious use of your time. If you are getting by on five hours of sleep a night, you may think you are unaffected by marathon work sessions, sleepless nights, or the incessant interruptions of smartphones; but it is your sleep-deprived brain that is telling you that. Hundreds of scientific studies and experiments could all be wrong, but I would never bet my life on it, or my health.

Proper Sleep Reduces Timewasters

From a personal productivity perspective, adequate sleep is critical. Sleep loss cripples our thinking, lowers our ability to focus attention on projects and tasks, attacks our executive functions including working memory and reasoning ability, and eventually debilitates our manual dexterity and motor skills.

Adequate sleep is essential to effective time management. Just as a lack of adequate communication might be the cause of interruptions and errors, so the lack of adequate sleep may be the cause of many time problems: writer's block, self-interruptions, procrastination, mental mistakes, poor decision-making, and a lack of creativity. That's why I often refer to adequate sleep as a "time management strategy."

In the process of presenting over two thousand workshops or speeches during my forty years as a speaker and trainer, I've learned that if I must sacrifice a good night's sleep before a time management presentation to review or memorize material, I opt for the sleep. You already have enough information in your memory bank on your chosen topic to do a good job. But when you are sleep deprived, you not only can't recall the material you recently studied, but you also have difficulty recalling information from your long-term memory as well. Lack of sleep can have a similar negative impact on writing.

Sleep has restorative and memory supporting powers. And if you agree on a holistic approach to time management, you must include adequate sleep among the strategies for improving personal productivity.

Proper Sleep Is Needed for Willpower

To maintain willpower, you must get plenty of sleep. Willpower is often highest in the morning and lowest at night. (Have you noticed that people stick to their healthy eating routine in the morning and stay away from sticky buns with their coffee, but grab an after-dinner bowl of ice cream?) Since willpower takes energy, food that gets converted to blood sugar can also improve willpower. Studies have shown that people's blood glucose levels drop after exerting willpower. So don't skip meals, take breaks during the day, avoid stress, and don't expend all your energy on marathon writing sessions. You will need willpower to resist distractions while writing, and to avoid being diverted to other things when checking email afterwards.

As explained by Wray Herbert in his book *On Second Thought*, if we are overtired and mentally depleted our brain switches automatically to its less effortful mode; it's just too difficult to crunch a lot of information and sort it intelligently if we lack the fuel for thinking.

David Rock, in his book *Your Brain at Work*, claims that the prefrontal cortex, the part of the brain responsible for thinking things through and making decisions, uses up metabolic fuel faster than people realize, and that we have a limited amount of energy resources for activities such as decision-making and impulse control. Making one difficult decision makes the next one even more difficult.

An article in the *New York Times* described the results of

this energy drain on a parole board's decisions. It reported that after examining more than 1,100 decisions over the course of a year, prisoners who appeared before the board early in the morning received parole 70 percent of the time; but those who appeared late in the day were paroled less than 10 percent of the time. Then there was the case where two prisoners who were serving the same sentence for identical crimes appeared before the parole board at different times of the day. The prisoner who was scheduled to appear in front of the parole board at 8:50 a.m. was given parole, while the other prisoner who appeared at 3:30 p.m. was denied parole.

Ruling on case after case throughout the day caused decision fatigue and warped the judgment of the board members. And fatigue can have a similar effect on writers if they do not manage their energy as well as their time.

Writers Are Prime Targets for "Thinksomnia"

In 2014, I introduced a phenomenon I call "thinksomnia" in one of my blog posts. I had spotted the word on a website that challenged people to form a new word by combining two other words and giving it a definition. The definition was something like "The inability to sleep because you keep thinking about the day's hectic events." It was a combination of the words "think" and "insomnia," and articulated perfectly the main idea in the article, in which I suggested that people are so busy the only time they have for creativity is just before falling asleep at night. The definition I usually apply to it is "The brain's attempt to gain closure on the day." (When we discuss the Zeigarnick Effect in the next chapter, you will understand its full significance.) But from the perspective of sleep, it's not wise to end your working day with a lot of loose ends. The brain is wired to be goal-oriented and likes to see projects and tasks completed. So, if there are things to be completed, record them on your to-do list, along with any new items, including ideas you plan to work on.

Your brain already has enough things on its mind. It is only 2 percent of your total body weight but consumes up to 25 percent of the oxygenated glucose and nutrients distributed by your body's circulatory system. At night it repairs and replaces old neurons, decides what's important to you and what isn't, and consolidates memories—not to mention keeping your heart ticking and your lungs oxygenated, and maintaining all of the other bodily functions that keep you alive.

Oh yes, and in the morning, it provides you with fresh insights on how your new book should end (which may have been keeping you awake as the so-called "thinking" part of the brain chugged along on one cylinder). And perhaps a creative idea—an "aha" moment as well.

Let the brain perform its nightshift duties. You can't expect it to solve problems when you're so stressed out and tired that you are unable to think straight when not fully awake and alert. We are programmed to spend about a third of our lives in sleep. It's not a waste of time. During sleep those waste products are washed away. Sleep keeps us mentally sharp, creative, and productive.

Your job at night is to relax. Let go of the day's activities and go to sleep. Sleep is as critical to life as the air you breathe. Don't trade it for anything, not even an attractive advance on royalties you may feel is at stake if you fail to submit those sample chapters on time. Those "dayshift" parts of the brain that you rest will be rejuvenated, while the other parts carry on their essential functions during the night. You will be mentally alert, creative, optimistic, and energetic in the morning. That's worth more than another night of anxiety mixed with preparation. Believe it.

We need six or more hours of sleep every night to be at

our peak, and that varies on the "more" side for some of us. That's sleep time, not bedtime. Less than six hours sleep, and you are sleep deprived, which means you will not be at your best. As mentioned earlier, your sleep-deprived brain may tell you the opposite, but thinking skills will be way below average, and useable writing output will plummet.

There are ways of freeing up your mind and getting a good night's sleep, and that's not by taking sleeping pills. You might want to look at my eBook, *Sleep: A Time Management Strategy*. It contains twenty-five suggestions based on science for a good night's sleep. Here are a few to get you thinking of how to improve your sleep:

> Keep the bedroom cool. Scientific evidence indicates that 65°F to 68°F (19°C) is the ideal temperature for sleep.

> Do not consume caffeinated drinks within six hours of bedtime. Caffeine can stay in your system for twelve hours. Avoid alcohol and cigarettes as well.

> Stick to a bedtime routine. Where possible go to bed and get up at the same time every day, including weekends. It helps regulate the body clock. When people try to catch up on sleep on the weekend, the quality of extended sleep is quite low.

> If you go to bed and are restless, don't stay in bed. Trying to force yourself to sleep reduces the sleep drive. Read a book, listen to calming music, or engage in relaxation exercises.

> If thoughts of all the things you must do or specific worries linger in your mind, write them down on paper so you can put them out of your mind.

> Don't fight the biological clock. To paraphrase Ecclesiastes, there's a time to work and a time to sleep. Don't confuse the two.

Chapter 11

So, What's New?

At this point in your reading, you may recall something I said about nonfiction books on a specific topic. If there are already hundreds of books available on that same topic, the reader expects something from your effort they haven't read before, such as a new idea or a different perspective, and one that they can use or relate to. So I set an expectation for this book, which is that you will discover something new with respect to the craft of writing that you haven't come across before. You may question whether what you'll find in these pages is relatable to you, because this book is based on my experience as a writer, and the most I have achieved in the field of writing is to become a part-time writer. So like the song says, what's new?

In this chapter I'll introduce a few things I discovered that fascinated me, which is the link between writing and brain science. I originally applied the information to time management, my chosen topic of study, and then to the process of writing that is relevant to all genres of writing.

But before I do that, here are a few things that you may not already know unless you have read the same books I have.

We all know that our prime time, based on our chronotype, is the time that we are at our peak energy level and alertness, and hence we should schedule our most pressing tasks during this period. And as I mentioned in chapter 3, I choose to write for ninety minutes in the early morning because I am up and out of bed early. Prime time varies according to the individual; we are not all on the same circadian rhythm. Some of us are larks or early birds, some are night owls, and the rest fall somewhere in between.

Mornings work great for me because of the nature of my genre—nonfiction. But it wouldn't necessarily be the right time for me if I become a novelist, according to research quoted by Michael Breus in his book, *The Power of When: Discover Your Chronotype—and Learn the Best Time to Eat Lunch, Ask for a Raise, Have Sex, Write a Novel, Take Your Meds and More.*

Breus points out that different activities require different traits or disciplines. For example, writing a novel requires creativity above all else, while writing a business book requires the processing of information. It may sound counter-intuitive, but efforts requiring creativity or insight should not be tackled in our prime time when we are most mentally alert, but rather during periods of low energy, when the science tells us we are at our most creative.

Breus backs up his information by describing a study conducted by researchers at Albion University where 428 college students were measured for their circadian preference, and then split into morning, evening, and in-between groups. They were then asked to solve three problems in each of two categories (insight versus analytical thinking) in both the morning and afternoon.

Based on their chronotype, students got more answers correct in the analytical category during their optimal prime time, but they solved more of the insight questions during their non-prime time.

For example, for the type of nonfiction work I publish, I require focus and the absence of interruptions or distractions. My best time of the day is early morning, when I am at my peak—what Cal Newport refers to as "deep work." Breus would probably agree with this, because I need to be focused, factual, and analytical as I attempt to provide instruction in a clear, concise, and coherent way.

Breus uses the example of authors of fiction, who require creativity and insight as they develop the plot and characters in a novel they are writing. He says they should *not* write in their prime time, whether that is in the morning, evening, or whenever, but rather when they are in the low energy part of the circadian rhythm. When they focus, however, as in editing the manuscript later, they should select their prime time. Breus says that memorizing, paying attention, decision-making, and planning are best done when you are the most mentally alert—in your prime time.

So, if fiction writers are early birds, they might choose a coffee shop in the late afternoon or early evening. As mentioned in chapter 3, a coffee shop environment also supports creativity. Breus agrees that the worst possible time for anyone to either focus or create is between 2 p.m. and 4 p.m. and from 12 midnight to 7:30 a.m. The latter time should be reserved for sleep, when your brain is consolidating memories and making remote associations that will aid creativity the next day. The ideal nap time would be sometime between 2 p.m. and 4 p.m. Of course, if you want to skip the nap and meet a deadline instead, head for the coffee shop. Cortisol levels dip at that time, according to Daniel Pink, in his book *When: The Scientific Secrets of Timing*, and coffee will give you a boost.

I suggest you decide whether your genre primarily requires either creativity or analytical, logical thinking and try scheduling the bulk of your writing time accordingly. I would think poetry, for instance, would be highly creative, as would fiction, but you are the best judge of that. My type of writing is best scheduled in my prime time in the mornings. But even if this were not true, I would continue what I am doing now because it would be difficult to consistently write for ninety minutes undisturbed at any other time of the day. Also, you will have noted that I write for ninety minutes before having breakfast. Pink recommends you delay having coffee one hour or ninety minutes after waking up, once your cortisol production has peaked.

You might try different times. When you find your "sweet spot" of writing time, you will know it. Do what works best for you. There are exceptions to every rule.

Take Advantage of the Zeigarnik Effect

You have probably heard of the Zeigarnik Effect. But it is also likely that you have not taken full advantage of it yet, so this section may also qualify as something new to you.

The Zeigarnik Effect is a psychological phenomenon that occurs when an activity that has been interrupted or left uncompleted is more readily recalled by people when compared to completed or uninterrupted tasks. This effect suggests that the tension in the brain created by an incomplete task makes its content more easily accessible and memorable.

The Zeigarnik Effect was first observed with servers in restaurants. They seemed to remember everything that each guest ordered without even writing it down, until the guests had been served. Then the servers quickly forgot who had ordered what.

Bluma Zeigarnik, a Russian psychologist, studied this phenomenon in the 1920s. Unfinished tasks are more securely held in your short-term memory, limiting additional working memory, and causing stress. When you switch to another task before the first one is complete, your brain is using up energy hanging onto the memory of the first unfinished task. When you ignore your email in the morning, part of your attention is on the unchecked, uncompleted email while you are working on your priority.

This phenomenon is somewhat like attention residue, which will be discussed in the next chapter, but while the Zeigarnik Effect is about memory, attention residue is about attention lingering on a previous task. Both cause stress, and the fear of missing out (FOMO) is another element that adds to the strength of this impulse to check email and the concomitant demand on energy, willpower, and short-term memory.

The brain loves closure, so it makes more sense to schedule enough time to complete all email messages at one or more sittings rather than flitting back and forth throughout the day. That's another reason I spend about a half-hour first thing in the morning checking and dispensing with my email before working for ninety minutes on my priority of the day, whether that is writing or a different project altogether. Then, after each ninety-minute work session, I spend another half-hour dispensing with additional email that may have arrived in the interim. That way fewer emails accumulate in my inbox, and the Zeigarnik Effect, attention residue, and retroactive interference (see chapter 14)—and of course FOMO—are reduced to a minimum. This break also provides an opportunity for renewal. Your performance increases when you have an uncluttered mind, just as it does when you have an uncluttered desk and office, so productivity is maximized as well.

You don't necessarily have to dispense with everything in your inbox. Scheduling a time to do it later or even adding it to a to-do list satisfies the brain's need for closure to a certain degree. But don't leave it hanging like meal orders in a restaurant waiting to be filled. There are other reasons why we should check our email in the morning, despite opinions that suggest otherwise.

Bluma Zeigarnik carried out a variety of experiments by giving participants a bevy of tasks to do and interrupting them during half of the tasks, telling them not to complete them. Results showed that they remembered the unfinished tasks between 50 percent and 90 percent better. Other researchers also found similar results. But variations were caused by such things as fatigue, the level of motivation to complete the task, and difficulty of the task.

Baumeister and Tierney, in their book *Willpower: Rediscovering the Greatest Human Strength*, suggests that one way to experience the Zeigarnik Effect is to start listening to a song, and then stop listening halfway through. The song will probably continue to run through your mind on its own at odd intervals.

The Zeigarnik Effect can affect productivity either positively or negatively. It shows that you can reduce procrastination by simply starting a task; once started, your brain will want to complete it. I have also used it to quickly recall where I left off writing when I'm working on a book or lengthy article. I simply decide on one final sentence before I quit for the day. Then I write only the first part of the sentence. As I start reading that sentence upon returning to my writing, the brain tends to complete the rest of the sentence and gets me back on track.

According to Daniel Pink in his book *When: The Scientific Secrets of Timing*, Ernest Hemingway also used the Zeigarnik Effect when ending a writing session. He didn't stop writing at the end of a chapter or paragraph but in the middle of a sentence. According to Pink, "That sense of incompletion lit a midpoint spark that helped him begin the following day with immediate momentum." Who knows? Maybe Hemingway got the idea from Bluma Zeigarnik, who first reported it in 1927. Hemingway wrote most of his books between the mid-1920s and the mid-1950s.

Hemingway called it "leaving water in the well." Kenneth Atchity, in his book *A Writer's Time*, published in 1986, refers to it as a "mechanical restart technique to create an automatic linkage between your writing sessions." He recommends that at the start of the next session you read the last few paragraphs, and by the time you get to that half-finished sentence you will have no trouble finishing it. I, in turn, got the idea from those books by Breus and Pink that I mentioned earlier. It pays to read a lot if you write a lot. That's how writers can prime the pump.

On its negative side, the Zeigarnik Effect could cause you to "multitask in your mind" if you have email messages waiting to be opened or people to call. These keep popping up in your brain, reducing your concentration and productivity. But knowing that you will be completing these things ninety minutes later when you take your next break reduces any ongoing effect to a minimum.

The Zeigarnik Effect also helps fiction writers to keep the reader engaged by introducing a cliffhanger at the end of a chapter. (But it might also leave readers upset if some characters are left with their problems unresolved by the end of the book.) This ploy can be used in nonfiction books as well if your desire is to keep the reader immersed in the book. But nonfiction readers often prefer to read more slowly, highlighting or underlining pieces of information, making notes, and "cherry-picking" those ideas that they feel will help them the most.

If you have a distasteful and unimportant task that you might have started but have no intention of finishing, cross it off your to-do list. Consider it finished. And be sure to keep an organized desk or writing area—one that is not filled with trophies and certificates of merit that might cause your mind to wander. "Out of sight, out of mind" is not a useless bromide.

How I Take Advantage of the Zeigarnik Effect

When I started the daily routine of spending the first half hour of the morning checking and responding to email messages, text messages, and voicemail messages from the previous evening, *before* starting my first ninety-minute work session, my productivity increased.

It is important to note that my ninety-minute work sessions, which are followed by brief breaks for coffee, a stretch or two, returning messages, phone calls, and "small stuff" are sessions which Cal Newport and others might call deep work, which you might recall is focusing on a specific predetermined priority while ignoring any would-be distractions. This means the iPhone is silenced, the landline has voicemail engaged, the door to your working area closed (if you have one), and you have resolved not to let your mind wander during the full ninety minutes or so that you are writing.

It's amazing how much you can get done in ninety minutes once you block the outside interruptions and develop your willpower to keep on task. And anyone can improve their willpower or self-discipline in the same way that Anders Ericsson discovered musicians could become top performers through repetition and deliberate practice. Stick to your desired routine and it will become habitual.

As far as interruptions are concerned, you cannot eliminate them, so why waste so much time trying to do so? The question should not be, "How can I eliminate interruptions? The question should be, "How can I be more productive in my writing?" The answer could be to have your potential interruptions delayed for ninety minutes. Seldom is anything that urgent that it couldn't wait ninety minutes. And if you're an early bird like me, you can complete a 150-page book in three months with no problem if you only write for ninety minutes every morning. If I can do it, almost anyone can.

Make the Zeigarnik Effect Work for You

The Zeigarnik Effect can even be used to promote a book that you are writing. For example, you could include excerpts from the unfinished book on your blog and/or post them on social media sites such as Facebook, X, and LinkedIn. Potential buyers will get a taste of the book's content without giving away too much.

If it's a nonfiction book, you could release these chunks of information as articles based on the book. Be sure to include the title, release date, and how it can be ordered. It could be a series of articles posted weekly, giving readers a glimpse of what they can expect, and leaving them wanting more. When the book is released, they will not forget that they want to buy it or that it contains information they would like to have.

When I started to write books I intended to self-publish, I would always send a mailing to current and potential customers offering a special pre-publication price. It included a description of the book, release date, and ordering information. The advance income helped pay for the printing when the invoice for "balance owing" arrived.

An intriguing book title, chapter headings that pique their interest, and a description that provides a useful fact or two with the promise of more, all help to increase anticipation on the part of the potential customer. And purchasing the book makes the experience complete for them.

The Zeigarnik Effect permeates our entire life, from the spaced repetition of remembering information and studying, to the urge to keep viewing that TV series. Our brain's desire for closure can either work for us or against us. It's up to us to choose.

Before closing this chapter, I want to mention that the Zeigarnik Effect is enhanced if you really love to write and you approach each writing session with eagerness and excitement. It motivates you to be consistent in your writing. The unfinished writing project can stimulate creativity and encourage the output of new and fresh ideas as you continue. And it also encourages you to keep writing the closer you get to the finish line.

Chapter 12

A Reader's Brain

Looking at writing from a neuroscientific perspective explains why some novels and books are more successful than others. They take advantage of how the brain is wired. For example, a reader's brain is wired to be attracted to stories. We crave stories. We have been captivated by story-telling from the time we were children being read to at bedtime to adults who never fail to catch the latest episode of a soap opera. Stories have been passed down from generation to generation since humans were capable of communicating. The more interesting the story, the more the reader's eyes are glued to the page. And using the Zeigarnik Effect to end each chapter with a cliffhanger urges the reader to read one more chapter, and the next, until the book is finished.

Our brain is also wired to take the path of least resistance to conserve energy. And it's often a lot easier to read an entertaining novel or short story than to wrestle with a book that is meant to educate, such as the ones I write. To the best of my memory, I don't recall my late wife reading any of my books, and my friends rarely do so willingly. My best friend says they are boring.

However, for those who write business or self-improvement books, you can still make use of the Zeigarnik Effect to a certain extent and add a little humor when it's appropriate. Make use of relevant and colorful stories as examples, and add interesting sidebars and anecdotes. But hopefully your topic is of sufficient interest regardless to capture the reader's attention and inspire them to keep reading. Their motivation is primarily to get information on topics that will help them improve in their work or succeed in their personal life. That purpose is the basis for the books I write.

Brain Science and Writing

Science doesn't change anything; it simply explains why certain things work the way they do. The most popular writers have a gift. They know instinctively how to capture the attention of their fans and keep them engaged. Others learn from other writers or through trial and error how to do it.

For example, readers like simplicity and shorter words, because easily understood words consume less energy. It's not that readers care that their brain is hard-wired to take the path of least resistance or they have a preference for active verbs instead of passive ones because their brain is more aroused by active words. Readers simply find that big words and passive verbs slow their reading pace and may disengage them from the story. Good writing engages the readers because it puts them smack dab into the middle of the story.

As science progresses and neurologists discover more

and more about how the human brain operates, researchers will provide information that will help writers select words that entice the reader and increase their enjoyment of a novel or poem. Writers can already do that to a certain degree with the combined use of electroencephalograms (EEGs) and functional Magnetic Resonance Imaging (fMRI).

In his book *Writing for Impact*, Bill Birchard mentions how scientists have found that specific verbs like "hit," "box," or "strangle" light up readers' motor neurons more than "fight," a general word of the same kind. (Motor neurons are cells in the brain and spinal cord that allow us to move, speak, swallow, and breathe by sending commands from the brain to the muscles that carry out these functions.) Birchard feels that "Scientists, in an attempt to understand the brain, have provided writers with a wealth of information for increasing engagement with the readers."

Lisa Cron has written two excellent books on gaining the reader's full engagement by applying neuroscience to your writing: *Wired for Story* and *Story Genius*. But don't spend so much time reading about how to write that you don't have time to do the writing. Personally, I pay more attention to how successful authors write than I do to what they are writing about. Learn from the masters of writing.

Empathizing with the Characters

There is another type of neuron that is important for writers to understand. Mirror neurons are cells scattered across our brain that reflect our surroundings, including the actions and feelings of others. **This empathy with others includes emotions.** If you cringe at the sight of someone getting hurt, or empathize with a friend who is grieving, or feel uncomfortable when a coworker is upset and anxious, blame it on these specialized brain cells.

The human ability to capture people's mood, pain, and grief explains why readers relate to a fictitious character. In *Wired for Story*, Lisa Cron mentions one study of subjects who underwent fMRI of the brain while reading a short story. The same regions of the brain lit up whether they read about an activity or experienced it themselves. It's imperative to make our protagonist and other characters come alive in the mind of our readers. **This enables readers to have a fair idea of why the characters act the way they do.** For example, when they grab a cup of coffee, a specific mirror neuron fires to tell them to reach out and grip the handle of the cup. And when they visualize a protagonist who is grief stricken over a loss, another neuron fires so they feel the same emotion as the character is feeling.

When you tell your story—at least when you tell it effectively—you create images in the minds of your readers, and it's as though those readers are taking on the role of the protagonist or hero of your story. They feel the same emotions as those you are describing in your book as the protagonist progresses towards their goal.

Talk about hooking the reader! They are not only observing but are fully involved and anxious to see what the main character will choose to do. As a writer, you are telling the readers not only what the main character and perhaps others are doing, but what they are thinking and feeling at the same time. It is a learning experience for the readers. Perhaps they can relate to the character's situation and don't know what they would do if the same things happened to them. Or they are silently urging the character to take a certain stance. In life, by simply observing someone, you don't know the reasons for certain actions they take. You can't read their minds. In stories, you make known the reasons and emotions involved in any action they do or don't take. As a reader, once you feel the emotion felt by the protagonist, empathy puts you in that person's shoes. You are adopting their emotions as the situation develops.

Roman Krznaric, in his book *Empathy: Why It Matters, and How to Get It*, suggests that the success of the book *Uncle Tom's Cabin* was aided by the author's ability to empathize with the African–American's experience of having their children taken from them and sold off to others. The author of *Uncle Tom's Cabin*, Beecher Stowe, was able to relate to this experience because of her experience of losing her own young child during the outbreak of cholera. Also, in his book *The Attention Merchants: The Epic Scramble to Get into Our Heads*, Tim Wu attributes the popularity of the *Amos 'n' Andy* radio program in the 1920s to the elaborate plot lines and empathy created with the happy, lovable characters portrayed.

And what made this emotionally possible were those mirror neurons, which we all possess. This reminded me once more of that editor's suggestion in a rejection letter that I should experience life before writing about it. That's certainly true of nonfiction as well and confirms my belief that you're never too old to start writing. I'm probably more capable of writing novels at ninety than I was at nineteen.

Readers Need to Know Why

Peter Mountford, a popular writing coach, mentions in an article on exploring emotion and conflict in the May/June 2024 issue of *Writer's Digest* that "Current thinking in psychology indicates that there are about ten basic human emotions—sadness, happiness, fear, anger, surprise, disgust, pride, shame, embarrassment, and excitement—and everything else is a blend of these basic ingredients."

The onus is on the writer to explain why characters in the story behave the way they do. I now realize why I failed at writing saleable short stories while in high school and college, and why one editor commented, "Also, the boy's change of heart on page 11 needs more explaining, and so does the brother's sudden appearance as a gang member." If a character suddenly has a change of heart, the reader must know the reason.

Lisa Cron points out that books tell you why someone does something, while life only says what someone did: "Your story is more revealing than real life."

Research suggests that we succeed at this task by virtue of those mirror neurons—those brain pathways that fire whether we're experiencing the stimulus or we empathize with someone else's experience. But it is up to us, the writers, to breathe life into our characters. Body language can help us do that. Lisa Cron provides examples of how to use body language to indicate to the reader what characters are really thinking or feeling in *Wired for Story*. She also talks about storytelling in her book, *Story Genius*. I heartily recommend you add these valuable books to your library.

If you want your protagonist to communicate to the readers and reveal their true feelings regardless of what they may be saying to other characters in the book, I recommend you pick up a copy of Joe Navarro's book *The Dictionary of Body Language: A Field Guide to Human Behavior*. The author spent twenty-five years as a special agent interrogating spies and other dangerous criminals and describes 407 behaviors in his book that help interpret an individual's true intentions or feelings. As you convey your characters' motivations, choose and describe behaviors that your readers are probably familiar with, and use dialogue to assist with character development.

Emotionally charged events persist much longer in our memories and are recalled with greater accuracy than neutral memories. According to John Medina in his book *Brain Rules*, "When the brain detects an emotionally charged event, the amygdala releases dopamine into the system. Dopamine greatly aids memory and information processing."

I hope people don't simply read your books but experience them as well. This involves creating protagonists that are relatable, warts and all. The reader's brain responds more to believable characters who have flaws like the rest of us. Have them behave in character. With the aid of the reader's mirror neurons and their familiarity with basic body language mannerisms, readers will experience what the characters are experiencing and become fully involved in the story, and be unable to put down the book.

Having said that, I wish I could do it. But I never returned to fiction because of my failure over sixty years ago. Since then, it's been nonfiction—educational, self-development, and business books. But it has been a great journey and it elevated my speaking and training career. When I fully retire, perhaps I'll have another go at fiction. After all, I'm more mature now and can handle rejection.

Chapter 13

A Writer's Brain

According to the book *Executive Functions and Writing*, edited by Teresa Limpo and Thierry Olive, executive function skills have been researched extensively during the past three decades. Proof of this claim is that between 2010 and 2019, 30,787 papers were published. There is no shortage of scientific papers that are pertinent to writing since it is an activity that follows us from the cradle to the grave. Much of the research has been focused on writing for academic purposes, as is the case in the above-mentioned book and in *Boosting Executive Skills in the Classroom* by Joyce Cooper-Kahn, who states that "writing may be one of the most complex executive function tasks students face in school."

Sometimes referred to as "habits of the mind," a person's executive skills are those brain-based skills (aka cognitive processes) required to execute tasks—that is, getting organized, planning, initiating work, staying on task, controlling impulses, regulating emotions, and being adaptable and resilient. These skills primarily reside in the prefrontal cortex, the part of the brain that helps you solve complex problems, achieve goals, and maintain self-control.

The potential for these executive skills is hardwired into your brain at birth, but the strength of each one as you age is determined by your upbringing, experiences, environment, and training. You can also inherit certain strengths or intentionally develop them. Different skills develop at different times, but growth is fastest during the infant and toddler years. Executive skills are not fully developed for twenty years or so—the last areas of the brain to fully develop. As with most strengths, you either use them or lose them.

People with weak executive skills are those who have trouble getting organized, managing their time, planning, and staying focused. They tend to be impulsive, are known to procrastinate, and get easily sidetracked. If a child had these characteristics, they would probably be diagnosed as having ADHD. Many researchers believe that ADD and ADHD are disorders of executive skills. All agree that if the child has ADHD, at least some executive skills will be impaired such as the ability to pay attention, stay focused and stick to one task for any length of time. And yes, ADHD can be diagnosed in adults as well.

The female brain is smaller but the prefrontal cortex matures about two years earlier, giving girls an advantage when it comes to executive skills such as sustained attention, self-regulation, and emotional control. This could be the reason why nine boys are referred to medical clinics for behavioral problems for every one girl, and why boys are three times more likely to be diagnosed with ADHD.

As an aside, if your children drive you crazy with their

reluctance to get up and at it in the morning or are forever putting off cleaning their room, remember that their executive skills are still under development while yours have matured. That's probably why it bugs you so much.

In business, it's not unusual for executives to hire an assistant who has the strengths that they lack. In the same way, your writers' group members may have different strengths than you have and could help you with editing or solving a problem with inconsistency in a character's actions. That's another advantage of belonging to at least one writers' group.

Executive functions or skills are necessary for everyday life, not just for managers, students, or writers. Weakness in any of these skills makes essential functions difficult for the individual, regardless of their age or vocation. So I will quickly review a few strategies for improving each of the twelve skills presented below. If you want to study them in more depth, there are several books listed in the references that discuss executive functions. The skills that I mention below are from the book *Work Your Strengths* by Chuck Martin, Richard Guare, and Peg Dawson. The authors focus on matching your stronger skills with tasks that require those skills, as opposed to offering tips on how to strengthen lesser skills.

As a general note, these skills are called for in tasks where success depends upon the degree to which an individual is capable of sustaining attention, manipulating ideas, resisting temptations, thinking before acting, and/ or dealing with unanticipated challenges. Any of these strengths is an asset for writers of any genre.

Twelve Executive Skills and Advice for Writers

Response Inhibition

Response inhibition is the ability to think before you act. Applied to writing, one example would involve thinking about your selection of words to describe a character's feelings or actions in a particular situation and not using the first words that come to mind. Pause and reflect. It's important that your character's words and behaviors are consistent with how you have initially portrayed them, unless there is a rational reason for a change in personality or behavior.

> ***My Process:***
>
> *I jot down chapter headings and list the topics to be covered, without paying much attention to the order I list them in. If I decide I don't have enough topics to satisfy a reader's curiosity, I usually decide to write a few articles instead of attempting a book-length work. But as I continue to accumulate more information, those articles could contribute to a book somewhere down the road.*

Working Memory

Working memory is the ability to hold information in memory while performing complex tasks, such as being able to keep several words or phrases in your short-term memory while you decide which ones you will use.

> ***My Process:***
>
> *Working memory is an important function for writers, and one that I sometimes struggle with when writing. If I start building a case for a point I want to make, by the time I do so I sometimes forget how I was going to express the point itself. That's when jotting things down as you think of them is important. In the same way, if I think of something that I should use in a future or past chapter, I*

immediately make a note of it. I don't want to waste time trying to recall it later or switching to another chapter when I'm fully engaged in the current one.

Emotional Control

Emotional control is the ability to manage emotions to achieve goals. For example, I flunked this one by being so upset at receiving a rejection letter containing suggestions for improving my story that I tossed the short story aside and tried a different genre completely. I have often regretted doing that.

My Process:

Anger, worry, and fear can be defused by positive self-talk. When you reason with yourself, you are using another brain function, neuroplasticity, to your advantage. Of course, as you mature, your emotional control usually strengthens. This reminds me of a remark made in a Hallmark movie: "Never let success go to your head, and never let failure go to your heart."

Sustained Attention

Sustained attention is the capacity to focus on a task despite fatigue or boredom. A weakness here might trigger writer's block, mind wandering, or a failure to focus on your writing for the amount of time you have set as your goal. The best way to improve this skill is to pace yourself.

My Process:

These time-wasters are rarely triggered in my case because of my habit of writing for only ninety minutes at a time without a break, combined with getting enough sleep and taking afternoon naps.

Task Initiation

Task initiation is the ability to begin tasks without undue procrastination. Many writers have suggested that the most difficult part of writing is getting started. I've personally heard dozens of times from individuals that they would like to write a book someday. For most of them, "someday" never comes.

> **My Process:**
> *This skill is related to goal-directed persistence and breaking the goal into small steps to achieve one at a time and feel good about. It is imperative to schedule blocks of time to write; what you are doing is setting appointments or meetings with yourself. If you fail to do so, your days will be consumed by what others demand of you. To-do lists, whether written or not, are simply intentional, but time blocked off in your planning calendar for meetings or appointments with yourself are commitments. People rarely miss doctor appointments or important business meetings.*

Planning/Prioritization

Planning/prioritization is the capacity to develop a road map to arrive at a predetermined goal. For someone writing a novel, this road map is an outline of a story or plots, and setting and character descriptions. For someone writing a nonfiction work, the road map could be an overview of the book and a chapter outline. There are exceptions where writers can develop a plot and characters as they go along, but it is easier to reach a goal when you have a plan in place, and the plan should be kept handy for reference.

> **My Process:**
> *I create an outline and a list of major topic ideas. I look for gaps in information that need to be filled in.*

The order in which topics is presented is critical to a reader's comprehension, so I assess whether the ideas are sequenced in a logical manner and is there connective tissue between them.

Organization

Organization is the ability to arrange materials according to a system. This involves everything from the arrangement of the books and working documents in your office or work area to the progression of a story or arrangement of the chapters in a book. Organization and time management are closely related, and according to the authors of *Boosting Executive Skills in the Classroom*, brainstorming and organizing ideas are two writing skills that support both creativity and clarity of expression.

My Process:

As I write about in chapter 6, whenever I think of a topic to write about, I label both an electronic and manila folder and start accumulating relevant information on that topic. Once I have decided on the topic I will write about next, I make up additional folders for chapter headings based on what I think should be covered in the book and separate the material into those corresponding folders. The material in each folder gives me ideas on what should be included. In addition to research, my experiences as a manager for twelve years, business teacher for eight years, and owner of companies, are rich fodder for topics.

Time Management

Time management is the ability to estimate and allocate time effectively. Carving out time to write, setting a schedule, and sticking to a plan is one of the most important executive skills for a writer. It involves knowing your chronotype and energy level, and fitting your writing time into the most interruption-free period of the day. Time management and personal organization go hand in hand, and I usually discuss them together.

> ***My Process:***
>
> *As I also write about in chapter 5, make commitments to write at scheduled times by blocking off time in your planning calendar. To-do lists are just intentions, while scheduled blocks of time are commitments. Predetermined starting times, including those ninety-minute blocks of time in which to do your writing, is a basic time management principle.*

Goal-Directed Persistence

Goal-directed persistence is the ability to have a goal and follow through until its completion. Saying to yourself, "I plan to write a book" is not a goal. It must have a start time and a finish time, and a writing schedule in between, always allowing more time than you think the project will take. If you choose not to set deadlines you can bet it will take much longer to complete your project.

> ***My Process:***
>
> *My goal is to write for at least ninety minutes a day every morning. It has become a habit, and over the last eleven years it has resulted in an average of four eBooks a year, and one self-published every two years, which is a level of goal-directed persistence that is fine with me.*

Flexibility

Flexibility is the ability to revise plans in the face of obstacles and setbacks. This refers to those times when you are disrupted from your normal routine because life happens. You can be pulled off-plan by an urgent family matter or having to have your laptop repaired. Remember how important it is to manage your emotions. If you can take things in stride and course-correct as needed, it shows you have strong flexibility.

> **My Process:**
>
> *Flexibility comes with experience, but it helps to have perseverance. If you want something badly enough, you will find a way to get it. I learned to roll with the punches as my early attempts at writing hit a brick wall. But I discovered that when you bounce off one brick wall, you can try a different one. When I failed at writing stories, I tried something different— short verse, epigrams, greeting cards, nonfiction articles, and finally books. The process becomes easier the longer you work at it.*

Metacognition

Metacognition is the ability to observe yourself in a situation and make changes so you're better able to solve problems. In other words, you can assume the role of CEO of your life, see that you work objectively, and act based on what needs to be done to produce a novel, novella, or book that readers will enjoy (and not necessarily one that mirrors your personal philosophy on life. Of course, if you are writing for yourself, not others, you can scratch that last comment.)

> **My Process:**
>
> *I discovered truth in the statement that you can't see the forest for the trees. Metacognition involves distancing yourself from your work or writing and viewing it as others see it, especially editors and publishers. Metacognition is exhibited by successful CEOs who oversee the entire corporation. The workers only see how their work impacts themselves. The managers see how it impacts their departments, but CEOs see how it impacts the organization.*

Stress Tolerance

Stress tolerance is the ability to thrive in stressful situations—perhaps "thrive" is a little optimistic. But if you have a high degree of stress tolerance you are able to go with the flow and not overreact to setbacks to the point they interfere with your health, productivity, and quality of your output. In stressful situations, your weakest skills fail first and become more pronounced.

According to the book *Work Your Strengths* mentioned previously, the executive skill that is the most significant in high performance is planning/prioritization. The top strength in the most high-performing males is metacognition. The top strength in most high-performing females is organization. And the most common weakness in both is task initiation.

Chapter 14

Strengthen Your Executive Skills

Sleep, brain exercise, balancing high-tech with high-touch, diet, reducing stress, and adding variety to your life will help strengthen your executive skills since they impact your cognitive skills in general. Adequate sleep is a must, and I have already included a chapter on its importance. Briefly, here are other ways of strengthening those executive skills.

Keep your brain active and strengthen neural connections by learning new skills. You might start by doing everyday tasks differently. Use your non-dominant hand to operate the computer mouse or open jars in the kitchen. Routinely using your non-dominant hand causes your neurons to fire differently.

Exercising your brain, even without moving from your chair, reaps physical benefits. Cleveland Clinic Foundation research has indicated that just *thinking* about exercising a muscle will strengthen that muscle.

In stressful situations, your weakest skills fail first

and become more pronounced. Fatigue and information overload tend to weaken them further. Avoiding, releasing or being able to manage stress is important. Also, you should assess your workload. Be organized, plan adequately, and allocate time to things of importance. Simplify if possible. Delegate and outsource. Pace yourself. Too much exertion without breaks taxes the executive skills.

Neuroscience has proven that the more you use a circuit in the brain, the stronger it becomes. The reverse is also true, so don't relinquish all your tasks to a computer. Training your memory, creative writing, or any skill can be strengthened through practice, but variety seems to be the key. Improving one executive skill doesn't necessarily improve all the others. Doing crossword puzzles only increases your ability to do crossword puzzles, and this holds true for most computer games as well.

There are exceptions, however. Exercise, for instance, stimulates the creation of new neurons not confined to the region of the hippocampus that stores new memories. Art Kramer of the University of Illinois at Urbana–Champaign found that a year of exercise can give a seventy-year-old the connectivity of a thirty-year-old. Harvard researchers have linked aerobic exercise with improvements in food choices and the ability to resist temptation. They feel it may inspire healthier choices by altering structures in our brains that deal with regulation and impulse control while also making us happier and calmer. This could account for weight loss in addition to the calories you burn through exercise.

Other activities such as meditation and certain video games can change brain structure so that brain processes are more efficient. Meditation has been shown to have a positive effect on the immune system and cardiovascular function as well as the brain. In one study, those who meditated showed less activity in the brain area associated with negative emotions such as anger and anxiety and more activity in those areas associated with optimism and confidence.

And learning a second language can sharpen many of the executive skills. Ellen Bialystok of York University in Toronto found that the workout the brain gets in bilingualism carries over to improve such skills as problem solving and attention switching.

Balance High-Tech with High-Touch

Paper Still Has Its Place

Balancing high-tech with high-touch can also strengthen executive skills. I suggest this could be done by introducing more paper into your life, which to most people might seem like a step backward. But I feel we moved too quickly and too completely into the digital world. It's as though our goal was not to increase productivity, but to eliminate paperwork. And for many of us, especially those struggling with weak executive skills, personal productivity decreased while stress levels climbed.

Using a paper planner, for instance, serves to ground me. I can touch it and feel it and see my scheduled projects the moment I open it. Writing down an appointment solidifies that meeting in my mind, while dictating it to a handheld device makes little impact, little commitment, and little chance I will even recall it the next morning.

A pen in hand generates focus, attention, commitment, and a "do it now" mindset (something many of us lack). Written down, a name or number stays in working memory longer and has a greater chance of making it into long-term memory for later recall. Fast is not necessarily better; it's just faster.

Similarly, I prefer making handwritten notes while on the telephone, jotting ideas on a steno pad instead of reaching for my smartphone or laptop, writing notes on an action sheet in meetings, and heaven forbid, even writing personal notes on hardcopy birthday cards and sending them by snail mail.

There is a place for digital devices. I do own a handheld device or two, a netbook, and a laptop, and like most people I do online banking, use e-transfers, make calls with Skype, shop online, have a PayPal account, participate in social media, and correspond by email. But I also use a paper planner and a hard-copy follow-up file system, a telephone log booklet, paper checklists, note pads and sticky notes. (And I still read paperback books.) Paperwork adds structure to my life, because paperwork *is* structure.

Because we live in a digital age of speed, I'm almost embarrassed to admit that I handwrite all my books and articles. But I quickly regain my self-esteem when I recall that story of the tortoise and the hare. The objective was clearly not to run the fastest, but to win the race.

Watch What You Eat

Diet is important for a healthy body and certain foods in particular have been found to be good for the brain. For example, blueberries are believed to reduce the risk of age-related diseases such as dementia and Alzheimer's. Avocados are thought to be good for the brain because of their monounsaturated fat, which increases blood flow through the brain and lowers blood pressure, and organ meats because they are high in brain-healthy nutrients such as vitamins A, B12, D, E, K, as well as folic acid.

Egg yolks are rich in choline. A shortage of choline has been linked to insomnia, memory problems, and fatigue. Egg yolks also contain ant-inflammatory omega-3s, as do salmon, herring, and sardines. Most nuts are also a source of vitamin E, which protects the brain's iron from exposure to oxygen. According to a special issue of *Newsweek* published in October 2014, 90 percent of Americans overlook vitamin E in their diet.

Any food that reduces high blood pressure or helps the cardiovascular system in any way is good for the brain since the brain's blood supply is critical. This includes such foods as oatmeal, brown rice, and grain breads.

> *I believe breakfast is the most important meal of the day. This is certainly true for me, since I expend a lot of energy before breakfast. For the last ten years or more I have stuck to the same breakfast routine. Thank goodness I love oatmeal. I add raisins, blueberries, flaxseed meal, cinnamon, honey, and banana slices. And 2 percent milk. I made up a chart listing each ingredient and the health benefits of each one.*

Break the Habit of Forming Habits

While habits are great for saving time and conserving mental energy, they are not so great for the brain. The same can be said for any routine behaviors to varying degrees. They provide little brain exercise. Driving the same route to work each day, having the same morning or evening routines, and doing tasks or activities in the same way again and again strengthen the neural links required for those pathways. But links to other pathways no longer used become weak. You may be getting the work done faster, but you are losing out on a lot of brain activity that could strengthen your executive skills.

There's nothing wrong with developing the habits of writing every morning and taking time off every other week, because the brain-stimulating variety is in the plans you develop, priorities that you work on, and leisure activities that you participate in. But don't get stuck in a rut or make your entire life a series of repetitive routines. This has the perceived effect of making the passage of time go much faster, as I discuss in my book *Slowing Down the Speed of Life.* I make the point that you won't be able to recall individual writing sessions if all of the sessions are similar in routine. The brain saves energy by simply recalling that you wrote every morning, but not the details of a particular article or who or why you might have been interrupted. With fewer details, your total life in retrospect will seem a little briefer than it was. That's another reason for not writing all day, every day.

Chapter 15

Managing the Brain's Time Wasters

While most people manage their time by organizing their office or writing environment, introducing time-saving apps and technology into their working lives, and increasing their efficiency and effectiveness by adopting the many suggestions of time management consultants, the brain has a mind of its own. It has already developed heuristics, which are mental shortcuts that make decisions faster and effortlessly, in addition to hard-wired habits that appear innate. Here are a few that either hinder or help us, depending on the situation, and how we can help them along or prevent them from slowing us down.

Brain Gymnastics

Multitasking

It is common knowledge that attempting to focus on two tasks at the same time with a view to doing them equally well is futile. The word "multitasking" is a misnomer, because despite the myth that it is possible to do two things at the same time, your brain will not agree. As efficient as it is, your brain is only capable of "task switching." Even computers can do only one thing at a time. It's just that they are so fast it appears the computer is doing many things simultaneously. And although the brain can become very efficient at frequently switching back and forth between tasks, there are consequences of doing so. It not only slows you down and decreases the quality of work, but it can also decrease your personal productivity by as much as 50 percent.

Dr. Theo Tsaousides, author of *Brainblocks: Overcoming the 7 Hidden Barriers to Success*, explains how shifting 100 percent of your attention from task to task requires a tremendous amount of energy and causes mental fatigue. He refers to what most people do as "serial multitasking"—continually moving 100 percent of your attention to another task, and then moving it back again—again and again throughout the day. Each time, you need to remember where you were with the original task while you transfer 100 percent of your attention to something else.

According to Gloria Mark, author of *Attention Span: A Groundbreaking Way to Restore Balance, Happiness, and Productivity*, it's never a clean switch when you go from one task to another, such as working for only twenty minutes or so on a task and then switching to another. The phenomenon called "attention residue" interferes. What happens is that when you switch from one task to another a residue of attention remains on the original task. Experiments have proven that this attention residue can cause poor performance on the next task. The more you switch back and forth from one task to the next, and the less time you spend on each one, the greater is the negative effect on performance and the more time consumed. That is one reason I recommend working for ninety-minute chunks of time on your projects, and not twenty-five minutes as suggested by the Pomodoro technique.

Ninety minutes is a reasonable time to maintain focus, and a reasonable time for would-be interrupters to wait for a reply. (Working in snippets of time in waiting rooms or on airplanes is not very productive. It's better than nothing, although rest and renewal might be a better option.) You have a lot more beginnings and endings if using the Pomodoro technique, and more occasions for attention residue to take place.

Retroactive and Proactive Interference

There are other phenomena related to attention residue, but they are distinct. Retroactive interference occurs when new information a person takes in interferes with the person's ability to recall previously learned information. It is believed to be one of the causes of forgetfulness, and being aware of retroactive interference is important when studying or memorizing information. For example, if you are studying a topic and decide to move onto another without giving the topic the amount of focus it deserves, what you had studied gets pushed aside by the new material. The consequence is that you will have difficulty recalling information about the first topic. Retroactive interference takes place any time you switch from one task to another.

Proactive interference is the opposite phenomenon. It occurs when old information interferes with the ability to retain new information. For example, when I was teaching memory training, most people could memorize a grocery list of ten items by linking them together in a story. But if I asked them to remember a second list using the same method, many of them mistakenly included an item or two from the first list.

A personal example of proactive interference happened to me whenever I tried to learn Spanish. (My son and his family live in Mexico.) When I review the days of the week in Spanish, my previously memorized high school French interferes, and my *Lundi, Mardi, Mercredi* get mixed up with my *Lunes, Martes,* and *Miercoles*. This problem would be much worse if I were to switch from studying one language too soon after practicing a different one. The same problem might occur when studying or memorizing any information that is somewhat like something you had already learned.

And like retroactive interference, it is more prevalent when switching back and forth between tasks is more frequent, such as when working on brief items from a to-do list. That's why I recommend writing for ninety minutes, and not just twenty-five minutes or less. And since you have already checked your email, you are keeping the impact of these brain-based phenomena to a minimum. The longer you leave your email unchecked, the more often your mind drifts to that unfinished email, and with each thought of it you experience attention residue and a flash of FOMO. And the Zeigarnik Effect, explained in chapter 11, will ensure that you do keep thinking about it. Oh, and did i mention that the Zeigarnik Effect with its intrusive thoughts of uncompleted tasks can also lead to difficulty sleeping? (I mention this in chapter 10.)

Tim Wu tells us in his book The Attention Merchants: The Epic Scramble to Get Inside Our Heads *how marketers seize control of our eyes and minds. We have all experienced the impact of habits—whether good or bad— in our lives. Some are good and some are bad. It could be checking email, Facebook, or shopping sites every few minutes, or spending hours a day playing computer games. While you do, marketers have your attention so they can sell their products or ideas.*

Back in the 1930s—and long before email, the internet, or social media—an American psychologist and social behaviorist named B.F. Skinner developed a theory of "operant conditioning." It was based on the observation that our actions are based on reward or punishment. Now, checking email isn't for most of us altogether a rewarding experience, but Tom Stafford, a cognitive scientist, explained our compulsion to check it anyway due to what is called the "check-in" impulse. It has since been shown that, contrary as it seems, unpredictability increases our urge to repeat something. We know we are only rewarded occasionally, so we keep checking so we don't miss the reward once it comes.

Checking email, shopping online, indulging in social media, and playing computer games can become addictive. And the most effective way of maintaining a specific behavior is with variable reinforcement. It makes sense. Would it be as much fun fishing if you caught a fish every time you dropped a line in the water? The book I mentioned earlier is warning us how marketers are stealing our attention.

FOMO aka the Fear of Missing Out

There is a modern term being used that explains the main reason we spend so much time on social media and email. It's an acronym—FOMO—the fear of missing out. It refers to the feeling or perception that others are having more fun, living better lives, or experiencing better things than we are. Research into FOMO suggests it leads to anxiety, depression, and unhealthy behaviors. It is rooted in envy of someone else's lifestyle, experiences, or possessions; the tendency to be angry or dissatisfied with one's own life; or the feeling of helplessness, stress, or lack of self-esteem.

A study in the *Psychiatric Research Journal* found that the fear of missing out was linked to greater social media usage. And when we visit social media sites, we tend to compare our own day-to-day lives with the highlights of others' lives. This introduces stress as well—another time waster.

FOMO can lead to excessively checking email, so it checks the box as a major timewaster as well as a drain on our emotions. This is especially true in the case of Facebook. People are forever posting photos of themselves reclining on some exotic beach, having fun at Disneyland, quaffing ale with a dozen smiling friends at an Irish pub, or cheering on their football favorites at the Super Bowl amid 75,000 other avid fans. It's enough to make some people feel deprived, depressed, and doubtful that they will ever experience the fun, success, and accomplishments that others are experiencing.

Seldom do we post our faults or losses on social media. For example, "I yelled at the clerk this morning and completely lost my cool!" Or "I came dead last in the potato sack race at the church picnic," or "I lost forty dollars at the slots on Tuesday. My wife hates it when I gamble." Or "Here's a picture of me with the only fish I caught. It's under the size limit but I kept it anyway. I'll tell the game warden that it's bait." Or in the case of writers, "My book has been rejected by sixteen publishers to date, and one editor said I should stick to my knitting." I have seen nothing about rejections or failures in the limited time I have spent on social media. It's all about book launches, successful sales, and never about taking years to finally finish a book and having to pay $7,500 to a vanity publisher.

TV marketers take advantage of people's FOMO by portraying people using a certain product and having a great time doing so, and with great success. It seems so easy, and so much fun! Others create a sense of urgency by indicating that we may miss out if we don't order by a specific time or date or take advantage of a special offer, and so on. That could lead to increased time consumption as well.

All the above phenomena could be lumped together into one big category called self-interruptions. But these internal self-interruptions and time-wasters are knee-jerk reactions, which were built into our brain for a reason. But we weren't born with a manual explaining what these reasons were or how we can eliminate or reduce the effect of those that we don't find useful in our current work environment. Based on what we have covered so far, I think it is justification enough to change the highly recommended strategy of "Never check email in the morning," to one of "Always check email in the morning." It eliminates the negative impact of the Zeigarnik Effect by completing the unfinished task of checking your email. It reduces the lost time through attention residue and retroactive and proactive interference every time you think about those unopened messages. It also satisfies your curiosity and your FOMO, allowing you to focus on your writing so you can do a better job in less time and with less stress.

Overcoming FOMO includes spending less time on social media and less time watching TV. It is also recommended that we focus on what we already have in life instead of what's lacking and keep a gratitude journal so we can focus on the good things in life. Also, to seek more personal one-on-one relationships, keep a journal of fun things to do, and make plans that further our own goals rather than trying to imitate others.

Instead of FOMO, maybe we should refer to it as FOMA—the fear of missing (out on) anything. Writers are guilty of increasing FOMO in their readers when their writing is so good that people can't resist turning the pages, but hopefully it's a rewarding type of FOMO.

Mind Wandering

Do you remember the expression, "I have half a mind to ..."? Well according to the researchers, when we are working, our mind is on the task only about half the time. In fact, Harvard psychologist Daniel Gilbert found that our minds are wandering 46 percent of the time. For example, you may be at your desk focusing on the screen in front of you, but your mind is somewhere else. Perhaps it's at the movie you watched the previous night or turning over the matters at hand for the meeting you must attend in the afternoon, or the jacket you want to pick up at the cleaners after work. It's called mind wandering, and scientists have been studying the phenomenon for decades.

It involves a spontaneous drifting of attention away from any task and towards unrelated thoughts. It is sometimes intentional, but it is more likely to happen if the project or task you are working on is not engaging or interesting enough to hold your attention. (Stop reading right now. Is your mind somewhere else?) But even if you are interested in what you are doing, the thought of unfinished email tends to pull attention away from the task at hand. And although mind wandering is not limited to serial multitasking where you are switching frequently from one task to another, another form magnifies its effect. Daydreaming is a form of mind wandering that involves acting out fanciful or wishful stories in your mind, and like other aspects of mind wandering, is a productivity killer.

Another Look at Thinksomnia

I discussed the origin of the term "thinksomnia" in chapter 10. Busy schedules and 24/7 connectivity tend to encroach on sleeping time. Most writers have experienced the impact of staying up late to finish a chapter of a book they are writing or to check emails before they call it a day—or should I say night. And when they finally get to bed, falling asleep can be difficult as they replay the day's events in their minds, mull over problems encountered or start thinking about all the things that they have yet to do. I refer to this as thinksomnia, an inability to fall asleep at night because of thoughts bouncing around in your mind when you should be relaxed and unburdened. I define thinksomnia as "the inability to sleep due to the brain's attempt to bring order and closure to the day."

The longer you work each day and the farther this extends into the evening, the greater the degree of thinksomnia you'll experience. Just as homework has been shown to have little or no academic benefits for elementary school children, working excessive hours has no benefits when it comes to quality writing output. But it does add more pressure to already stressed-out writers and infringes on family time, helps put their life out of balance, and fans the flames of workaholism.

When a reporter interviewed several winners of the MacArthur "Genius Grants", most said they kept cell phones and iPods turned off when in transit so they could use the downtime for thinking. That's what most people are lacking. Research shows that people think more creatively when they are calm, unhurried, and free from stress. Time pressures lead to tunnel vision.

Business executives who work sixty hours a week and make work a priority are called workaholics. It's true. And when I was teaching full-time and burning the midnight oil getting my business started at the same time, I was hospitalized with bleeding ulcers. That's what finally woke me up to the fact that health should be the priority, not work.

But when writers put in sixty hours a week, they are applauded as creative and prolific writers, destined for stardom. Don't believe it. Creativity doesn't emerge from an exhausted brain. So pace yourself. You will have fewer instances of mind wandering. Fortunately, one thing that makes you more resilient is to love what you are doing. And most writers are passionate about what they do—but don't push your luck.

Chapter 16

Publish First—Get Paid Later

When I started writing articles, the objective was to promote my speaking business, not necessarily to earn money. So I chose to target trade journals—those smaller-circulation magazines that focused on specific industries or business functions such as leadership, marketing, travel, and so on.

The trade journals listed in *Writer's Market* are mostly those glossy, high-quality publications that pay well and as such are inundated with submissions. In contrast, the trade magazines that were more receptive to unsolicited submissions, and less critical of writing ability, were listed in *Canadian Advertising Rates & Data (CARD)* for Canadian publications and *Standard Rates & Data Service (SRDS)* for American publications. These publications continue to be an excellent resource for looking up small trade journals (by inference many of which were excluded from *Writer's Market*). The downside is that these trade journals seldom paid the writers. I suppose writers chalked it up to experience and something to have on their resume. I made good use of *CARD*.

Writing for Trade Journals and Controlled-Circulation Magazines

As I mentioned, I published several magazines: *The Ceramic Hobbyist, Canadian Clay & Ceramics,* and *Sales & Marketing Management in Canada,* which I owned, and *The Canadian Manager,* which I published on behalf of an association. They were all controlled-circulation magazines and all were listed in *CARD*. (Controlled-circulation magazines are mailed free of charge to their target audiences and may only have few paid subscribers.) As publishers, we seldom paid for articles submitted to us, but I always had a small stream of submissions from writers who would write for the sake of the byline—plus, of course, the credibility and visibility for their business or products they were marketing.

Professional speakers and other entrepreneurs who knew about them were after the "tear sheets" so they could include copies of their articles in their promotion kits that went to potential clients. (Yes, they have more influence than a business card.) As a publisher, I would at times edit news releases so they appeared to be articles since I couldn't afford to pay for freelance articles (much to the delight of the companies submitting the releases.)

Evidently I was not the only one who carried out this practice. According to Marcia Yudkin, author of the book, *6 Steps to Free Publicity,* the *Wall Street Journal* editor Frederick Taylor once admitted that as much as 90 percent of its daily news originates in self-interested news releases.

CARD and *SRDS* were very expensive at the time. An annual subscription to *CARD*'s print publication was about $600. Today the publication is digital and now it seems that they have transitioned their listings to a comprehensive online platform rather than publishing a monthly magazine. This platform provides a vast database of media properties and advertising data which is continuously updated and accessible online. You might find an old paperback copy at your local library or you can contact *CARD* or *SRDS* and check out the rates for accessing their databases.

But a less expensive way to reach these trade publications might be just to google "trade magazines" and see what you get. I tried this to see if it would get results. As I live in Canada, I googled "Canadian trade magazines." Up popped "Magazines Canada," and when I clicked on it I got "Member Directory," which provided links to over two hundred magazines. I googled one at random—*Canadian Horse Journal*—and discovered the publication does accept submissions, both fiction and nonfiction articles, poems, cartoons, etc. And the magazine will negotiate payment. Writers' guidelines are posted on its website.

I also googled "Canadian Professional Associations" and found a "List of Professional Associations," and among the hundreds listed I saw the Canadian Institute of Management and its magazine *The Canadian Manager*— the very magazine I once published for them when I owned an association management company decades ago. The association offers guidelines for submissions; for example, it accepts articles of 750 to 1,500 words. It points out it does not pay for the articles it publishes. It is now a digital quarterly.

The point I am making is that by spending an hour or two online you can collect a list of low-paying or no-paying controlled-circulation magazines that will make it easier for you to get published. There is probably a lot less competition than the prestige publications listed in *Writer's Digest*. And since you are only offering first North American serial rights, it does not prevent you from submitting the articles elsewhere after a reasonable length of time. In addition, you can still reuse the material in a book if that's your intention.

Most of the smaller magazines are open to a phone call asking whether they publish articles from freelancers. Call the editor. In many of these magazines the editors and publishers are the same person. When I owned my trade magazines, I used to list office staff members as circulation manager, advertising manager, etc., just to make the publication more presentable to advertisers, but I did a lot of that work myself.

And I was always scrambling for brief articles to include—ones that didn't cost me anything. If you happen to be an entrepreneur, you should take advantage of your writing skills and promote your business this way. Brief 500 to 800-word articles are suited for most trade publications, association magazines, and newsletters.

To make a profit, magazines must have at least a 30-70 percent split respectively between space for editorial and space for advertising. Controlled-circulation magazines require even a higher ratio of ads to editorial due to a lack of subscription fees. For example, if I only had eight pages of ads, the magazine would run to only sixteen pages. Subtract the cover, contents page, etc., and I probably had space for five pages for editorial content. How would listing only two or three articles on the contents page look to readers and advertisers? Not very impressive. I needed to have five or six articles to offer more substantial editorial content to make the magazine more appealing.

You could be a magazine editor's best friend. There are thousands of controlled-circulation magazines, including association publications and newsletters, looking for good, brief articles that are relevant to their readership. It's a win-win situation, but you must know where to find them.

Other markets for your articles are local newspapers and newsletters. I once submitted an article to a community newsletter, *The Cornell Crier*, which was distributed at the time to 9,000 residents in a newer community in Markham, Ontario. By the time all of the phases of the housing complex were completed, there were about 30,000 people. That's quite an increase in readership. I also was published in several newsletters.

Several times I had an article from a non-paying magazine picked up by a larger publication and received payment for it. Another time my son, who was attending college, pointed out that I was quoted in the management textbook on his reading list. The authors of the textbook had quoted text from an article I had published in a supervisor's magazine. I've had a couple of brief items picked up by *Reader's Digest* and other magazines as well. Overall, I have been quoted in books several times, mostly sourced from time management articles I had placed in small, non-paying publications. So never underestimate the power of the published word, payment or no payment. It sure helps your credibility should you decide to market yourself as an entrepreneur.

Sometimes you don't even have to submit articles to a publication. Simply post them on your website and on social media and you have a good chance of having them reposted and reprinted at other websites or in newsletters and house organs—with your permission of course.

There are plenty of websites that will accept your articles. Do a google search using the words "submit articles" and see the results. Be sure to read the writers' guidelines and agreement first. You don't want to agree not to submit them elsewhere as well. The name of the game is to get as much exposure as possible.

Don't forget one of the biggest advantages of writing articles—it forces you to write. While you are developing your writing skills, you are accumulating material that you can use in books, training programs, or high-profile consumer magazines.

Having said all that, the *Writer's Digest* is an excellent directory for magazines, trade journals, and association publications. Getting published in these offerings is competitive because writers are compensated. I have two *Writer's Digest* books in my library that are invaluable, not just because of the markets listed, but because of the articles and other resources listed as well. They are the *2018 Deluxe Edition* and the *2021 100th Edition*.

Books, Articles, or Both?

If you are only a part-time writer like me, I want to suggest how you can promote your main business with articles only.

If you are writing a book for the sole purpose of building credibility and/or promoting your business, consider writing articles instead. A great book might never be accepted by a major publisher, and self-publishing is expensive. Also, according to 2023 statistics, the average self-published book sells 250 copies. Could you sell more copies through a top publisher's self-publishing offshoot? You might find the cost either acceptable or prohibitive. In any case, if your intent is to reach potential clients, consider that you can reach infinitely more people by placing articles in dozens of small controlled-circulation magazines that have thousands of readers each.

For example, our *Canadian Clay & Ceramics* magazine was mailed to all members of the Canadian Ceramic Society, as well as to non-member companies who were involved in ceramics in some way, such as glass manufacturers and their suppliers.

Advertising revenue came from those companies wanting to reach the target market that the publication served. Entrepreneurs who sell their services to companies in almost any industry, whether it is travel, education, automotive, or whatever, might do well to submit articles to these trade magazines. This includes professional trainers, organizers, consultants, graphic artists and, of course, writers. If you are a prolific writer, just think of the number of 800-word articles you could write in the time it takes to write a 50,000-word book that may cost $5,000 or more to self-publish. If you were successful in having your work published in *People* magazine or the *AARP Bulletin*, you would reach over 22 million people. Imagine millions of people reading your byline, perhaps along your with company name, website, or email address.

Press Clipping Services

I would not have known the power of publicity if I hadn't subscribed to a press clipping service. In those days the service was available for a small monthly fee and I had them clip any items appearing in print media that mentioned my name or the name of my book, along with the words "time management." I had at least one hundred clippings sent to me over a two-year period. They were mailed weekly by first class mail by Bowdens Clipping Service.

I included copies of a few of the best ones in my press kit. Whenever anyone requested my availability and speaking fees, they would receive a copy of one or two articles as well. It's not that I was a better speaker than others—I didn't come close. But exposure pays off.

Clipping services are still available, and have expanded to include online, print, broadcast, and social media. The news clipping services are now sometimes referred to as press clipping services or media monitoring. If you want to know what online and print media have to say about you, your business, products, services, or books, you might investigate these services. The prices vary. Google News Alert, which is limited to online publications, monitors logs, newspaper articles, etc., and is free. Other services that offer more comprehensive coverage come with a monthly subscription.

But first, you should make sure you have material to monitor: articles, books, blog, social media postings, newsletter, or whatever. If you know anything about anything, don't keep it a secret. Send your press kit to TV and radio stations and invite the media to attend your workshops or speeches. (In this case, clear it with your sponsor if you have one.) I once prepared a time management workshop for members of the press and invited them to attend free of charge. I gave them all a press kit in addition to the workshop notes. When I was vacationing in Florida, I contacted the producer of a talk show on TV and told them about my latest book and asked if their viewing audience would be interested in time management. They said yes, and I was also invited back for another interview after my next book was published.

I scheduled brief early morning workshops at no charge and sent flyers to businesses in the area. That resulted in product sales at the back of the room and a few bookings for in-house workshops at local companies. Eventually I started charging for these workshops. I exhibited my books and time management products at conferences. I marketed a free monthly time management newsletter by subscription only, and when it reached five hundred subscribers, started mailing my product folders to them.

Much later it went digital, and even now I periodically send newsletters to over 2,000 subscribers.

It's great to have passive income from books, publications, and products. But passive income requires active promotion, and no one is more involved in promoting your book than you or your designated publicist.

Chapter 17

Writing Is Cathartic

Do you find that writing is cathartic? I certainly do. Many times as a youngster I would write about my failure to land a date with a girl I admired or my failure to succeed at having an article published and so on. It was usually in the form of a poem, which was never written to be published. It released any negative emotions inside me and gave me relief by having expressed it on paper. I'm sure that talking it over with someone would have worked as well, but I was always reluctant to share my failures with others.

I know nothing about catharsis except it is a psychological term for releasing repressed emotions. But I do know that writing poetry makes me feel a lot better about difficult situations, and brightens a good day even more.

Writing about positive experiences can also help our well-being, such as keeping a journal or diary or, as some writers have suggested, each day writing down three things that you are thankful for. I used to write many poems and essays with no intention of having them published. They were just to get the anger or frustration or disappointment out of my system. For example, here's a poem I wrote in my early twenties. And now it will see the light of day for the first time since I typed it on my old 1926 Underwood typewriter. It's called simply "You," and starts with a one-line stanza followed by progressively longer stanzas, using the same rhyme throughout.

You

Who warms my heart with her friendly smile?
You do.

Who strips my mind of its shroud of gloom
by simply being in the room?
You do.

Who makes me dream far into night,
not dreams of hate, or dreams of fright,
but dreams of life and strange delight?
You do.

Who, in some strange, uncanny way
breathes life into each dying day,
and makes me ponder with dismay
how fast the past has slipped away?
You do.

Who makes the world seem so serene
despite the sorrows that I've seen,
and though too late to change the scene
and turn dead leaves of love to green.
Who makes me think what might have been?
You do.

The poem might not be worthy of publication, but I decided to give it life by including it in this book. It's the least I can do for a poem that had a therapeutic effect on my life long ago. Another poem, written for an entirely different occasion, but with a similar sad, frantic rhyme, was meant to get emotions out in the open where I could deal with them.

Dear God

Dear God, I need you here beside me
To ease this horrid ache inside me.
I need your hand to gently guide me
Through this raging storm of life.

Dear God, my love is torn asunder
Was it me who made the blunder?
Is it really me, I wonder
Why I'm losing my dear wife?
If so, I've paid for all my erring
With this agony I'm bearing,
And I swear I'll not stop caring
If our marriage you will save.

For now, I know how precious love is:
Precious like your home above is
But also fragile like a dove is:
To be cherished to the grave.

Dear God don't leave me in my sorrow.
Let your light shine on the morrow.
Just this once please let me borrow
The hand that wipes away all pain.
Give back the reason for my life here.
End the strain and all the strife here.
God, touch the heart of my dear wife here
And turn her back to me again.
Amen

All emotions aren't sad, morose or morbid, however. I have written poems that were from frustration, fear, or simply for fun. Here's one written while I was in class at university. It expresses the frustration of attending a course called "Principles," and our frustration was compounded with the fear of failing (which most of us experienced at one point or another). Writing the poem was an attempt to provide the desperately needed release from anxiety and stress through humor. (At least it was meant to be humorous.)

Principal Worry

Hail to those Invincibles who understand Principles.
Hail to those talented few.
Those lads and lasses who lived through the classes
That Doctor Hines can construe.

My brain is all muddled, I'm stymied, befuddled
Without any nerve.
My mind is so bent it will never present
An equilibrium curve.

May all the races hear how our faces
Obtained their greenish texture.
Here you our fate as I relate
A typical Doctor Hines lecture.
No look of prudence appears on the students
as the master walks in.
And with an Einstein feature on the face of the teacher
the lecture begins.

"Now alpha minus beta is equal to Theta
If Theta is fared
With consideration for the concentration
And becomes one minus alpha 'C' squared.

"But the resulting reaction depends on the fraction
Of moles they display.
Thus, the occasion that ionization
Be replaced by the constant called 'K.'

"Now if the normal solution has some slight pollution
Due to impurity,
There's a small alteration in the neutralization,
Which makes the pH equal three.

"Now you take the cosine, any questions? No, fine.
Then you divide it by two.
But that's by the way. We'll do that next day.
"Now, here's a small problem to do:

'If sodium chloride and formaldehyde
Were mixed with a little malt,
And alpha squared minus Theta was equal to Beta,
What is the price of the salt?'"

Thus ends our class but alack and alas,
We are really mixed up, you can see.
The only way we could pass is to turn on the gas
And pass away silently.

So, hail to those Invincibles who understand Principles
Hail to those prides of the schools:
Those lads and lasses will surely get passes,
But God help the rest of us fools.

My apologies for the gross scientific inaccuracies of the poem's content, but after all, most of us did flunk the course.

Of course, there were other occasions where I fell in love with a gal who was already spoken for, and I had to wrestle with ethics as well as common decency. Love is such a powerful emotion, as expressed here.

To a Girl Not Mine to Love

I saw your face amid a sea of faces,
A wave of warmth surrounded by the cold.
But frequently such beauty's warmth erases
The coldness, letting happiness unfold.

And thus, it was for me that day in meeting,
When, saddened by the world, I saw your face,
And tried to steal some hope, however fleeting,
And warm my heart with embers of your grace.

But as happiness thrived on the sweetness of your smile,
And I sensed the love that welled within my heart,
Like avaricious man, I thought awhile
That I could have the whole, not just the part.

But God has ways of telling paltry man
He cannot possess what he doesn't own.
When God bestows a gift on someone else,
All others are to leave that gift alone.

So, saddened by a loss not mine to lose,
And resentful of a joy not mine to share,
In sleep, I walk in someone else's shoes,
And awake, I share humanity's despair.

I see your face amid a sea of faces,
A wave of warmth surrounded by the cold.
And chilled by the warmth that it embraces,
The love that's in my heart remains untold.

I write poetry now more for enjoyment than catharsis. My emotions all seem to be positive these days, so my last poem explains why I now live in a small town, Sussex, New Brunswick, instead of Toronto, Ontario. You hopefully can sense by the pace and rhyme that there are no regrets in this situation.

Romance in Old Sussex Town

*It was here in Sussex town where I longed to settle down
With my sweetheart who I met far, far away.
She drew me to the place with a smile upon her face
For she knew that I would settle here someday.*

*Now I'm a city man; taking subways when I can,
Rapid transit was the only way to go.
Never cared for grass or trees 'cause they only made me sneeze,
And the country life was just too dog-gone slow.*

*And Sussex seemed so bare, with no skyscrapers there,
No Sky Dome, CN Tower or CNE.
It seemed so strange to me, breathing air I couldn't see,
And even stranger that the parking spots were free.*

*But within a week or two of taking in the view
And breathing in the unpolluted air,
Fishing in the streams, fulfilling boyhood dreams,
Not living here just seemed too hard to bear.*

*So now I'm settled down in this little country town
With its murals and its agricultural fair.
And if you're thinking too that there's little here to do
There's hundreds of adventures I could share.*

*I know I tend to boast of the striking Fundy coast,
And the rugged nature trails along the way.
And it isn't hard to see why it's here I came to be
But I think I like who brought me here the most.*

*Her name is Esther Perry, and at first I was quite wary
Since she was a country girl all through and through.
We met in Florida by a pool, and she really seem quite cool,
And keeping in touch just seemed the thing to do.*

So, we emailed and we wrote, for I couldn't sing a note,
But I wrote a poem or two — or maybe three.
I visited once or twice, and my, she seemed so nice
That I decided to move to Sussex you can see.

Toronto's in my past and I am free at last
To do whatever I am led to do.
But one thing I will say, who really made me stay
Is the lady I just introduced to you.

And regardless of the weather, we are always seen together
Whether fishing or relaxing without fuss.
And it seems our favorite past time — and
it never is the last time
Is traveling on Nancy Drury's bus.

I've had a trial or two that Esther's seen me through,
If I haven't told you yet, she's quite a nurse.
She's taken me with urgency to the hospital's emergency.
Kidney cancer, double hernia, and worse.

One time with cellulitis and concussion just to spite us
And brain surgery of course was touch and go.
Without her speed the surgeon said, I
would have been quite dead,
And I would never have reached ninety as you know.

Bur Esther's been a blessing with her bandages and dressing,
And her kindness and her thoughtfulness as well.
And to our God goes the glory for this Cinderella story,
And I kinda love this lady, as you can tell.

Writing poetry now is something I do for special occasions
like birthdays and weddings, and whenever I get the urge.
I've collected samples that I have written from nineteen
to ninety, but none has been submitted for publication. I
did submit quite a few short verses as fillers as mentioned

previously. I suppose that's two more uses for writing: to entertain your family and friends, and simply because you love to write.

Last Words—for Now

When I started to write the introduction to this book, I was a few weeks on the "good side" of ninety. As I start to write the conclusion to this book, I'm several weeks on the "other side," and I find that it is just as good as the so-called "good side." The only difference is that I feel even more grateful for the time and experiences that God has allowed to come my way.

I enjoy many small things that I ignored so many years ago. I enjoy the fact that I wake up each morning. I used to complain that I hadn't slept well. I enjoy watching the rain attacking the windows or the snowflakes making silent landings on sidewalks outside, and the wind bending the trees. I used to grumble about the weather.

I enjoy getting text messages from my grandkids and seeing them on FaceTime, and meeting friends on Zoom. I used to lash out at all the spam and the younger generation's fascination with technology.

I'm thankful, not only for the things I can still do, but for the little things I accomplish that didn't mean much to me in the past. Occasionally, I pick up one of my humorous studio cards and think about the laughs it must have generated as it was displayed on the greeting card racks for thousands of people to see. I used to think only of the fifty dollars I received for writing it.

Perspective changes as we age. When I sorted through old files while writing this book to recollect the stages of my speaking career, the meaning of those items changed—a copy of a testimonial letter telling me how my workshop had changed an attendee's life, for instance. I had only seen it as praise, and something I could use to promote my workshops. But as I read it now, I think about the person, and the problems they must have been enduring. And the pleasant thought that something I had said improved the situation.

There is another point I want to make as we come to the end of our time together. Whether we are writing or speaking, we had better choose our words carefully. What we say could impact the life of a reader. A reader's life is far more important than selling another book or earning another few dollars. Whenever an article or filler or book was rejected, my disappointment had centered on the potential income or ego gratification or praise that publication might have brought me. Now I think of the potential readers, and my concern is focused on how my book might have helped someone. That reward for me is far more important and motivating than money. I suppose that's why volunteering is so rewarding. The money factor has been removed. Money has never been more than a short-term motivator. But in the long term, volunteering extends your lifespan.

Remember the 10,000-hour rule mentioned in chapter 2? The rule states that 10,000 hours is "the average number of hours of practice that the best violinists had spent by the time they were twenty."

According to neurologist Daniel Levitin, "Mastering

anything, whether you are a violinist, writer, speaker, or hockey player takes a lot of time and effort. It takes our brains that long to assimilate everything it needs to know to achieve true mastery." But it will vary with the individual, the field of endeavor, and the degree of focus—what is called "deliberate practice."

Well, I don't think, at my age, that I want to spend 10,000 hours attempting to become a top performer at anything. But there is another rule derived from research as well. It is not as well known, and I have only seen it mentioned in a few books. But it also has research to back it up. It's called the 100-hour rule and it involves being of service to others—volunteering. We don't have to practice for 10,000 hours to reap the benefits.

One hundred hours of service is the average number of hours of volunteering needed before the personal rewards come to be recognized. This phenomenon is described by Adam Grant in his book *Give and Take*. A study of more than 2,000 Australian adults in their mid-sixties revealed that those who volunteered between 100 and 800 hours per year were happier and more satisfied with their lives than those who volunteered fewer than one hundred hours. Only two hours of volunteering a week increases your happiness, satisfaction, and self-esteem.

Another study of several thousand Canadians revealed that for the first few hours a week, volunteers gained knowledge and skills at a consistent rate. The Exeter Medical School correlated evidence from forty different studies over the last twenty years and concluded that volunteering led to lower depression and increased well-being.

A study by the Harvard T.H. Chan School of Public Health revealed that older adults who volunteer for as little as two hours per week have a substantially lower risk of early death. This study, which included nearly 13,000 participants, indicated that volunteering helps individuals become more physically active and improves their sense of well-being, thereby enhancing longevity.

Isn't it interesting how being of service to others with no expectation of pay or gain of any kind, does, in fact, offer important rewards such as health and well-being, happiness, slower cognitive decline, and even longevity?

In my time management workshops I would have referred to volunteering as a time management strategy. It expands the time that is available to complete more of your personal and organizational goals.

One of my goals is to keep writing, so I keep volunteering. This year I'll be helping start another writers' group in my home town— one that is open to all who have an interest in writing and would like some workshops on techniques, a library of resources, and fellow members who are willing to share ideas and help one another, all at no cost to group members. Meetings will take place at the local library.

I also plan to continue my volunteering at the church I attend, our friendship club, the seniors' center, our new writers' group—and anywhere else that does not interfere with my allotted time for writing. And much of my writing is voluntary as well—the devotionals, my blog articles, my poetry, and my time management newsletters. But in the background, my writing is still working for me generating passive income.

I have no intention of relinquishing my ninety minutes of early morning writing. I can't think of a better introduction to the day.

I wish you a fulfilled and happy life. And make sure you schedule time to write about it.

Sources and Bibliography

Atchity, Kenneth. *A Writer's Time*, 1986.

Attenberg, Jami. *1000 Words: A Writer's Guide to Staying Creative, Focused, and Productive All-Year Round*, 2004.

Baumeister, Roy F. *Willpower: Rediscovering the Greatest Human Strength*. Penguin, 2011.

Bennett, Arnold. *How to Live on 24 Hours a Day*. Doubleday & Company, 2010.

Bick, Dee. *The Ultimate Guide to Writing & Publishing*. Filament, 2014.

Binchy, Maeve. *The Maeve Binchy Writers' Club*. Anchor Books, 2010.

Birchard, Bill. *Writing for Impact: 8 Secrets from Science that Will Fire Up Your Readers' Brains*. HarperCollins, 2023.

Bolles, Richard N. *What Color Is Your Parachute?: Your Guide to a Lifetime of Meaningful Work and Career Success*. Ten Speed Press, 2022.

Brett, Regina. *God Never Blinks: 50 Lessons for Life's Little Detours*. Grand Central Publishing, 2011.

Breus, Michael. *The Power of When: Discover Your Chronotype and Learn the Best Time to Eat Lunch, Ask for a Raise, Have Sex, Write a Novel, Take Your Meds, and More.* Little, Brown Spark, 2019.

Burkeman, Oliver. *Four Thousand Weeks: Time Management for Mortals.* Allen Lane Canada. 2021.

Butler, Octavia E. *Bloodchild and Other Stories.* Seven Stories Press, 2005.

Byrd, Virginia A. *I'm Still Writing: Women Writers on Creativity, Courage, and Putting Words on the Page.* St. Martin's Press, 2023.

Carter, Christine. *The Sweet Spot: How to Find Your Groove at Home and Work,* 2015.

Colvin, Geoffrey. *Talent Is Overrated.* Nicholas Brealey, 2016.

Cooper-Kahn, Joyce. *Boosting Executive Skills in the Classroom: A Practical Guide for Educators.* Wiley, 2013.

Coyle, Dan. *The Talent Code: Greatness Isn't Born, It's Grown.* Random House, 2020.

Cron, Lisa. *Wired for Story: The Writer's Guide to Using Brain Science to Hook Readers from the Very First Sentence.* Ten Speed Press, 2013.

Cron, Lisa. *Story Genius: How to Use Brain Science to Go Beyond Outlining and Write a Riveting Novel (before you waste three years writing 327 pages that go nowhere).* Ten Speed Press, 2016.

Csikszentmihalyi, Mihaly. *Flow.* HarperCollins, 2009.

Currey, Mason. *Daily Rituals: How Artists Work.* Alfred A. Knopf, 2021.

Dimitriadis, Nikolaos, and Alexandros Psychogios. *Neuroscience for Leaders: Practical Insights to Successfully Lead People and Organizations.* Kogan Page, 2021.

Ericsson, Anders. *Peak: How to Master Almost Anything.* Penguin Random House, 2016.

Fitzgerald, Isaac. *Dirtbag, Massachusetts: A Confessional.* Thorndike Press, 2023.

Gilbert, Daniel Todd. *Stumbling on Happiness.* Knopf Canada, 2009.

Gladwell, Malcolm. *Outliers: The Story of Success.* Back Bay Books, 2019.

Grant, Adam. *Give and Take: Why Helping Others Drives Our Success.* Penguin Books, 2014.

Hari, Johann. *Stolen Focus: Why You Can't Pay Attention.* Bloomsbury Publishing, 2023.

Harper, A.J. *Write a Must-Read: Craft a Book that Changes Lives—Including Your Own.* Page Two Books, 2022.

Herbert, Wray. *On Second Thought: Outsmarting Your Mind's Hard-Wired Habits.* Tantor Media, 2010.

Kadavy, David. *100-Word Writing Habit: A Small Action with Big Results,* 2023.

Keller, Gary and Jay Papasan. *The ONE Thing: The Surprisingly Simple Truth behind Extraordinary Results.* Bard Publishing, 2012.

King, Steven. *On Writing: A Memoir of the Craft.* First Edition, Scribner, 2000.

Krznaric, Roman. *Empathy: Why It Matters, and How to Get It.* Perigee, 2015.

Lakein, Alan. *How to Get Control of Your Time and Your Life,* 1975.

Lang, Amanda. *Power of Why.* HarperCollins Canada, 2014.

LaRocque, Paula. *The Book on Writing: The Ultimate Guide to Writing Well,* 2013.

Leist, Laura. *Eliminate the Chaos at Work: 25 Techniques to Increase Productivity*. Wiley, 2011.

Limpo, Teresa, and Thierry Olive. *Executive Functions and Writing*. Oxford University Press, 2021.

Mark, Gloria. *Attention Span: A Groundbreaking Way to Restore Balance, Happiness and Productivity*. Hanover Square Press, 2023.

Martin, Chuck, Richard Guare, and Peg Dawson. *Work Your Strengths: A Scientific Process to Identify Your Skills and Match Them to the Best Career for You*. American Management Association, 2010.

Medina, John. *Brain Rules: 12 Principles for Surviving and Thriving at Work, Home, and School*. Pear Press, 2014.

Navarro, Joe. *The Dictionary of Body Language: a Field Guide to Human Behavior*, 2018.

Newport, Cal. *Deep Work: Rules for Focused Success in a Distracted World*. Grand Central Publishing, 2016.

Partnoy, Frank. *Wait: The Art and Science of Delay*. Public Affairs, 2012.

Pink, Daniel H. *When: The Scientific Secrets of Perfect Timing*. Canongate, 2019.

Rock, David. *Your Brain at Work: Strategies for Overcoming Distraction, Regaining Focus, and Working Smarter All Day Long*. Harper Business 2020.

Ruffin, Maurice C. *The Ones Who Don't Say They Love You: Stories*. Random House, 2021.

Schwartz, Tony. *The Way We're Working Isn't Working: The Four Keys to Transforming the Way We Work and Live*. Free Press, 2010.

Schwarz, T. *Time Management for Writers*. Writer's Digest Books, 1988.

Sivertsen, Linda. *Beautiful Writers: A Journey of Big Dreams and Messy Manuscripts—with Tricks of the Trade from Bestselling Authors.* BenBella Books, 2022.

Taylor, Harold L. *God-Centered Time Management.* TaylorinTime, 2023.

Taylor, Harold L. *Making Time Work for You: A Guide to Productive Time Management.* Harold Taylor Time Consultants, 1998.

Tsaousides, Theo. *Brainblocks: Overcoming the 7 Hidden Barriers to Success.* Prentice Hall, 2015.

Waitley, Denis. *The New Dynamics of Goal Setting: Flextactics for a Fast-Changing World.* William Morrow and Company, 1996.

Westerhof, Patricia. *The Canadian Guide to Creative Writing & Publishing.* Dundurn Press, 2023.

Wilbur, L.P., and J. Samsel. *How to Write Articles that Sell.* Allworth Press, 1999.

Writer's Digest. *Writer's Market.*

Wu, Tim. *The Attention Merchants: The Epic Scramble to Get Inside Our Heads.* Knopf, 2020.

Yudkin, Marcia. *6 Steps to Free Publicity.* Career Press, 2009.

eBooks by Harold L. Taylor

Time Management for Authors & Writers. Bookboon, 2024.

Always Check Email in the Morning, and Other Brain-based Strategies. Bookboon, 2024.

How to Be a Top Performer. Bookboon, 2023.

How to Write Articles for Self-Promotion. Bookboon, 2017.

Sleep: A Time Management Strategy. Bookboon, 2015.

Strengthen Your Brain's Executive Skills. Bookboon, 2015

Boost Your Memory & Strengthen Your Mind. Bookboon, 2014.

About the Author

Harold Taylor, the owner of **TaylorInTime.com**, has been speaking, writing, and conducting training programs on the topic of effective time management for over forty years. He has written dozens of books, including a Canadian bestseller, *Making Time Work for You,* originally published in 1981.

During his career, he developed over fifty time management products that were sold in thirty-eight countries around the world. His time management newsletter, now in electronic format, has been published for over thirty-five years and he has had over three hundred articles accepted for publication in various magazines and newspapers.

A past director of the National Association of Professional Organizers, Harold received their Founder's Award in 1999 for outstanding contributions to the organizing profession. He received the CSP (Certified

Speaking Professional) designation in 1987 from the National Speakers Association in the U.S. In 1998, the Canadian Association of Professional Speakers inducted him into the Canadian Speaking Hall of Fame. And in 2001, he received the Founder's Award from the Professional Organizers in Canada. The award has been renamed the Harold Taylor Award.

Prior to his speaking and writing career, Harold held management positions in industry for twelve years at Canadian Johns Manville and American-Standard and was a teaching master in the business division of Humber College in Toronto for eight years. He has been an entrepreneur for over fifty years, incorporating four companies during that time.

His first company, Harold Taylor Enterprises Ltd., established in 1967, was an association management company that also published four magazines and a line of greeting cards, and sponsored public seminars and management training programs. Since 1981, when he incorporated the time management company Harold Taylor Time Consultants Inc., he has personally presented over two thousand workshops, speeches, and keynotes on the topic of time and life management.

Harold lives in Sussex, New Brunswick, Canada. He writes eBooks for Bookboon (forty-four to date), publishes a biweekly blog article on his website (also posted on Facebook LinkedIn & X), a free quarterly time management newsletter for his two-thousand-plus subscribers and, until recently, a "Business Matters" column in a local newspaper, *King's County Record*. He also speaks to seniors and other groups on "Growing older without growing old" in addition to "time and life management." His website is **www.taylorintime.com**.